GODS AMONG US

Macrophilia

and

Muscle Worship

Art Compilation

By: Jason Bushaw

This is a work of fiction. Names, characters, places, and incidents either are the product of the author's imagination or are used fictitiously. Any resemblance to actual persons, living or dead, events, or locales is entirely coincidental.
Every image contains images of men only aged 18+.

All illustrations and art copyright © 2022 Jason Bushaw

Book cover design copyright © 2022 Jason Bushaw

Independently published September 2022

ISBN 9798353291664 (paperback)

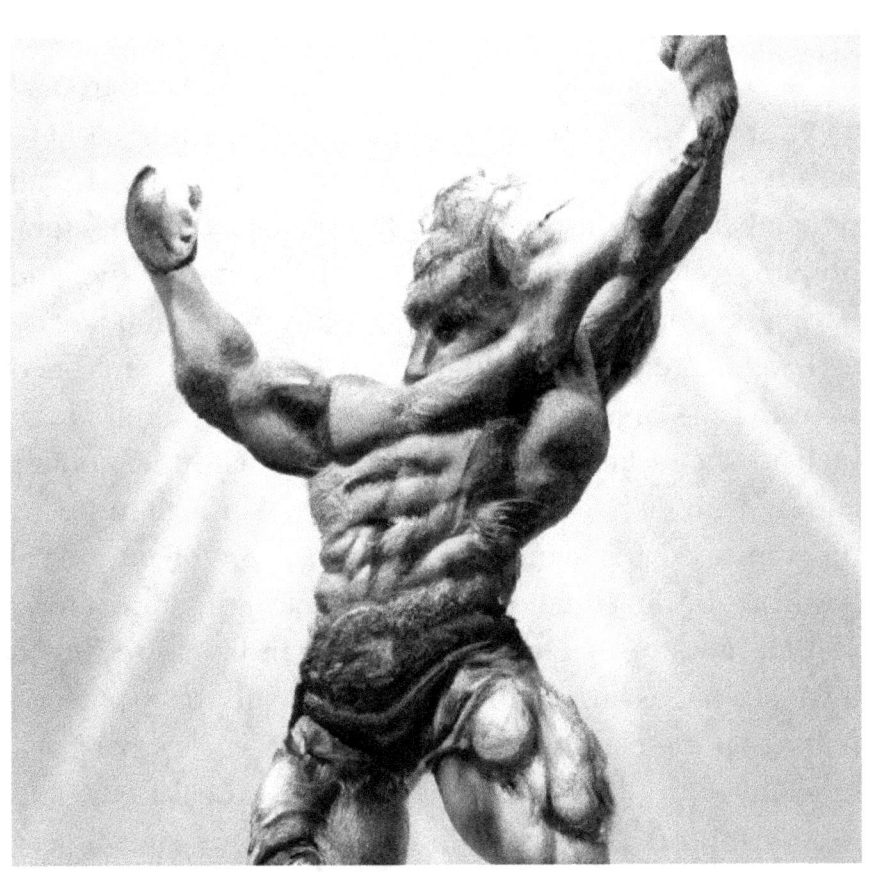

For the Love of Men

Hello, my name is Jason and I think we share something in common. We both love muscular men and muscle worship. I want to give you a type of introduction to my work, so you understand where my art originates from - and also so we can connect. Since I can remember I have admired muscular men. It started as a child. I can remember a few dreams of crawling on a larger man, sitting on him, feeling the density of his muscles around me, and having skin on skin contact. These dreams became fantasy as I went through puberty. The first men that I imagined were huge - larger than life men. Gigantic. I admired the men in shows like Hercules and Superman, their power and strength hit me in a very sexual way. Through my teens this remained the same and took up many of my sexual thoughts. In my adulthood it turned into lust, and I found real life ways to live out fantasy. I began lifting weights in my teens but as an adult I joined a gym and really pursued putting on muscle mass. There is a whole science behind it called hypertrophy. I started befriending muscular guys and fostering those relationships no matter if it was straight, gay or bi. I would go out to bars and find the most jacked guy and befriend him. You cant let fear from stopping you from meeting guys like that. I bet I will later write a novella about how to be Alpha and attract muscular men. I also travelled and used my charismatic skills to meet guys that looked huge - they looked like muscle gods! Tall, thick, masculine. Some were into the same fantasy as me. This is what I want for you, faithful reader, I want my work to inspire you to seek these men out and finally live out some of your favorite sexual fantasies.

In this book you will find some of my favorite creations (there are plenty more that are unpublished). As you will tell, I put more effort into some and less in others. I used pencil drawings mostly, and ended with digital art. I hope that you can connect with my material and create your own fantasy's.

Thank you for allowing me to share this with you.

Jason

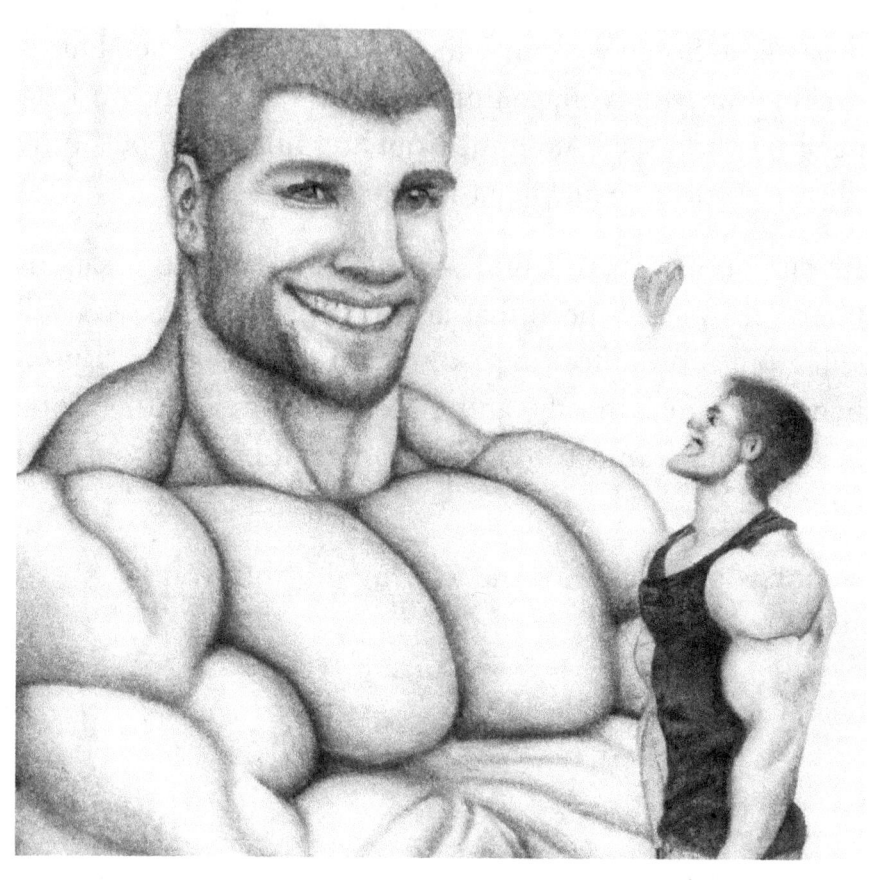

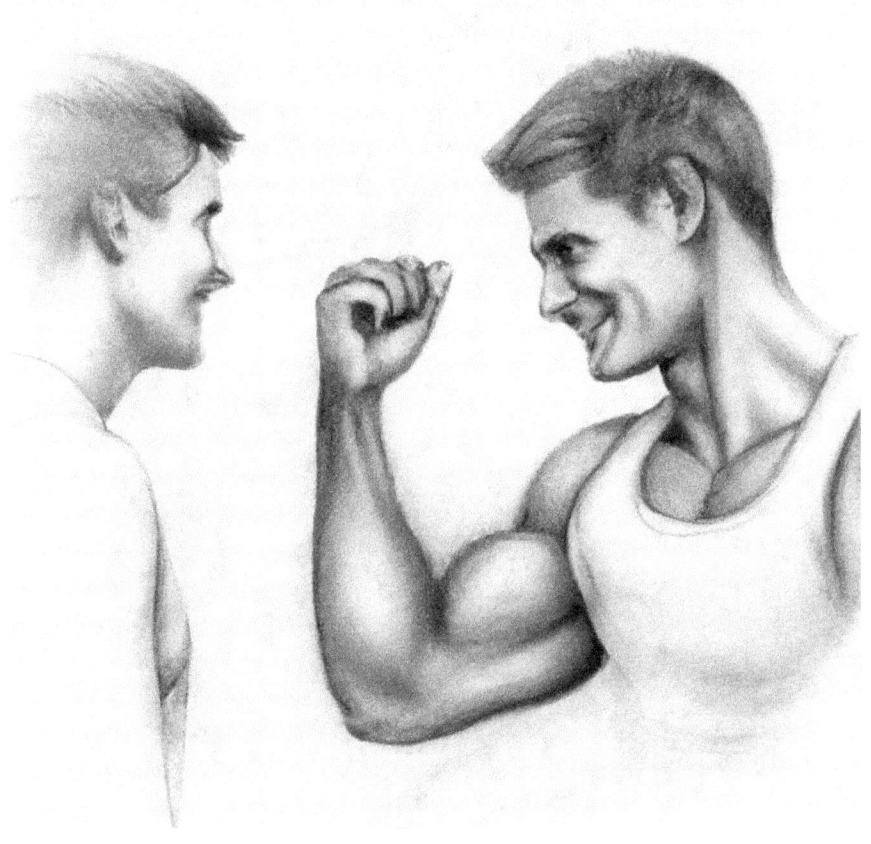

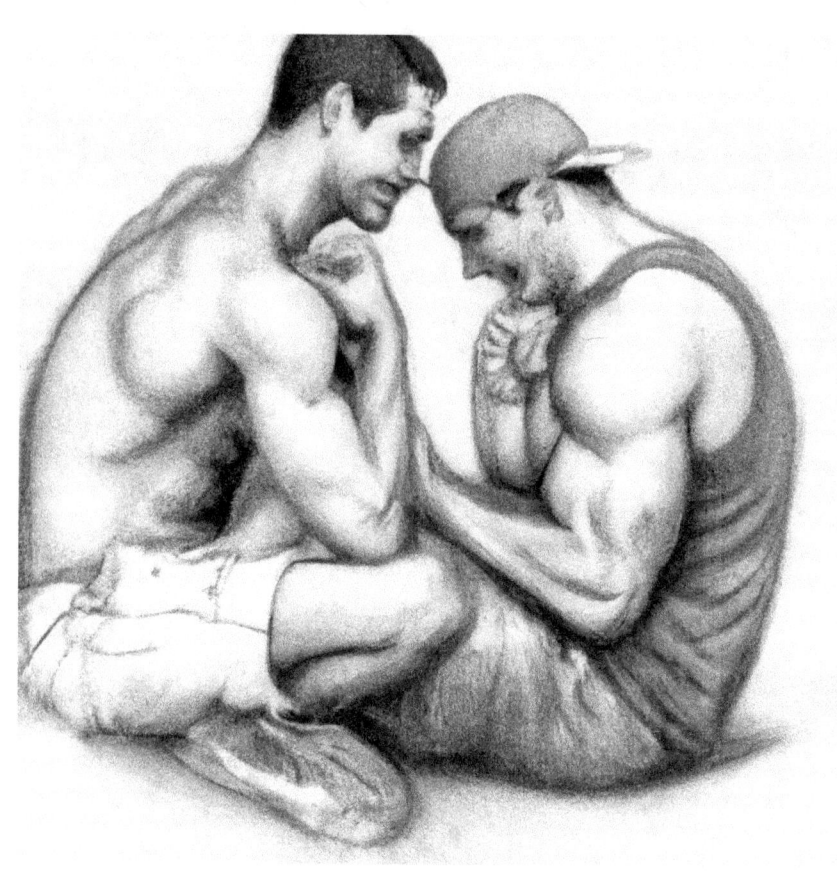

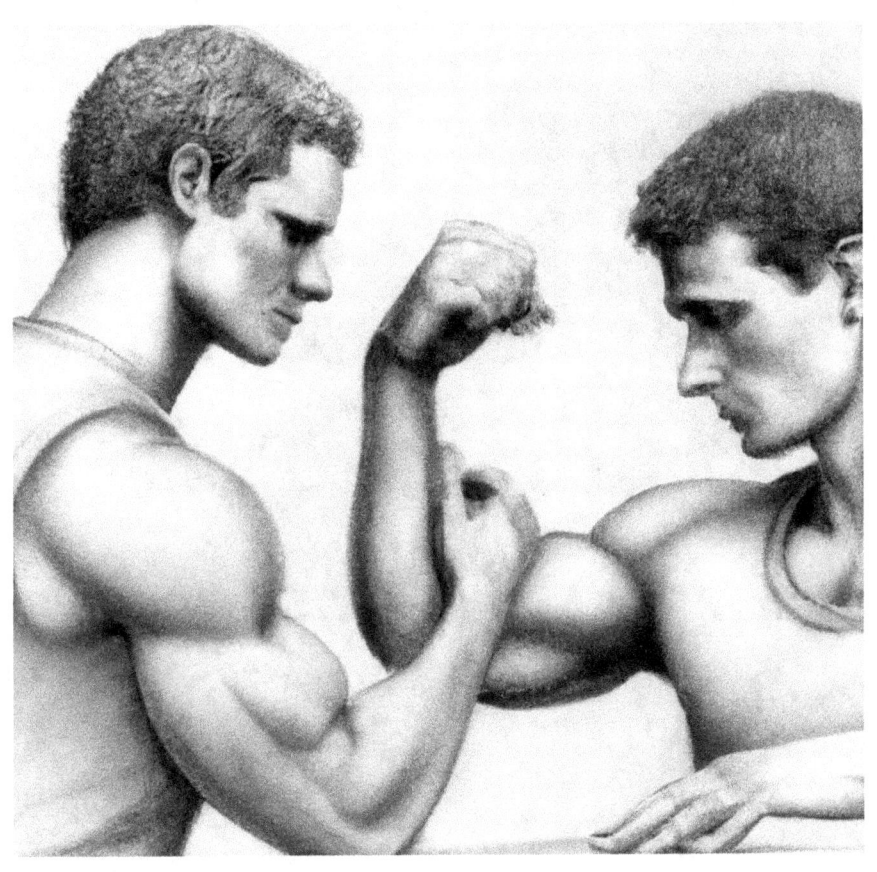

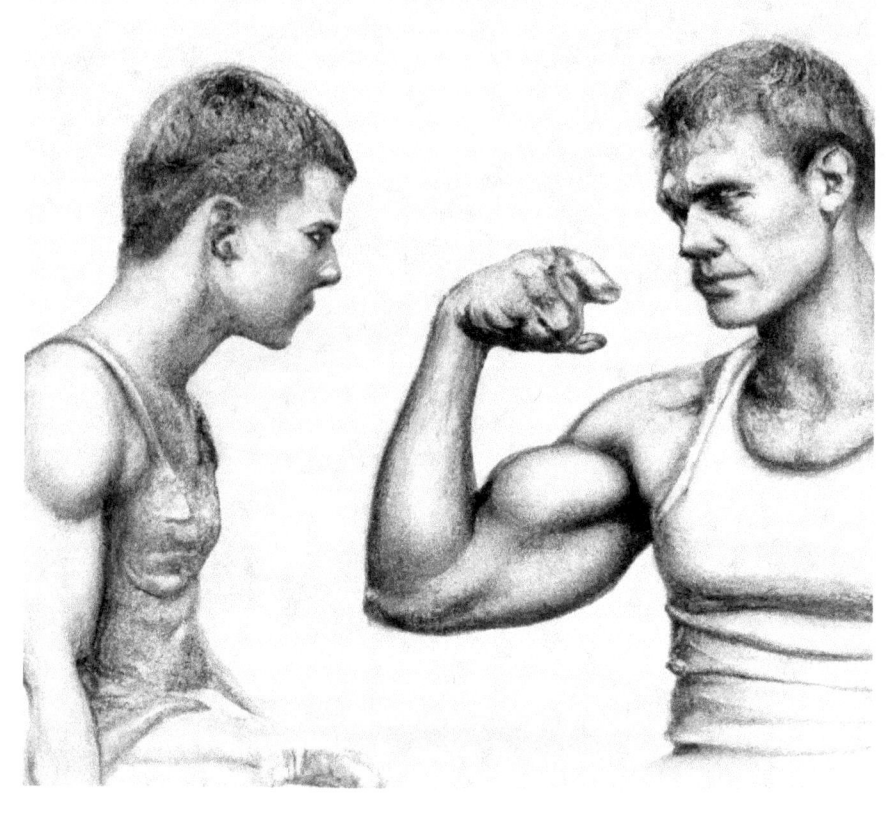

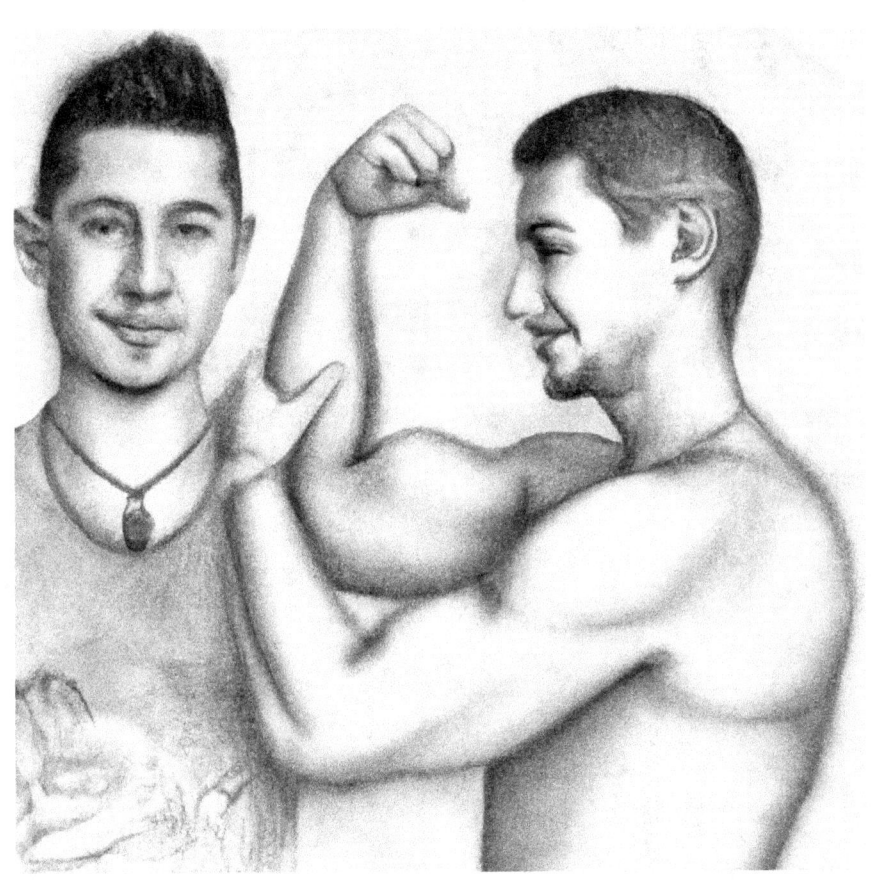

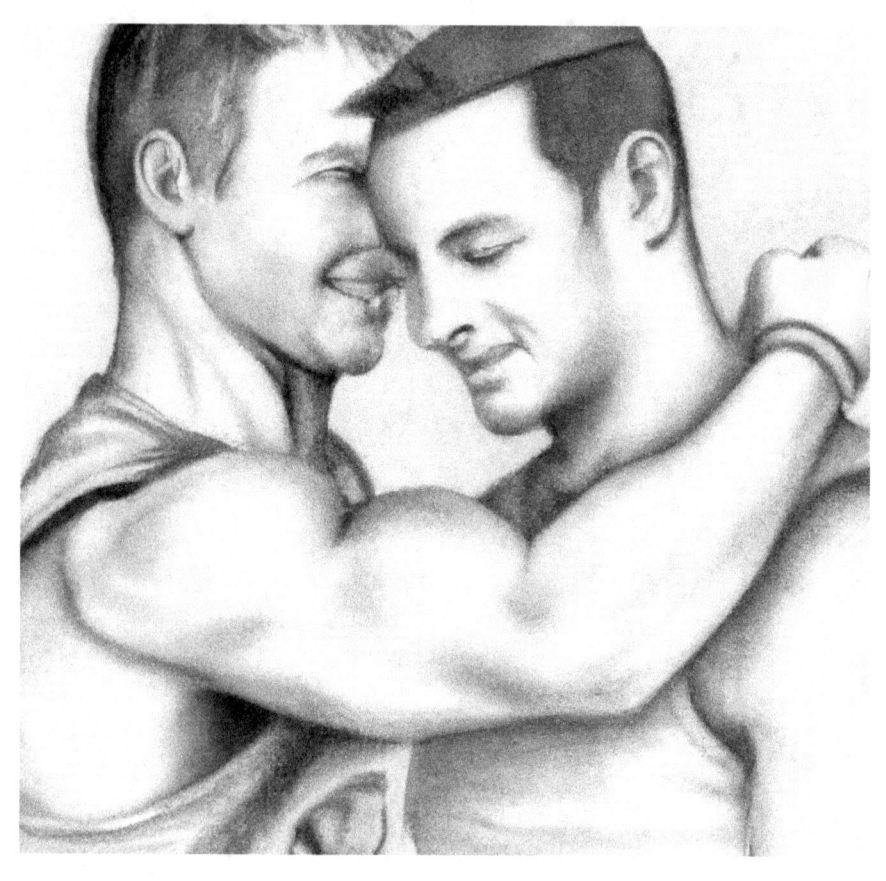

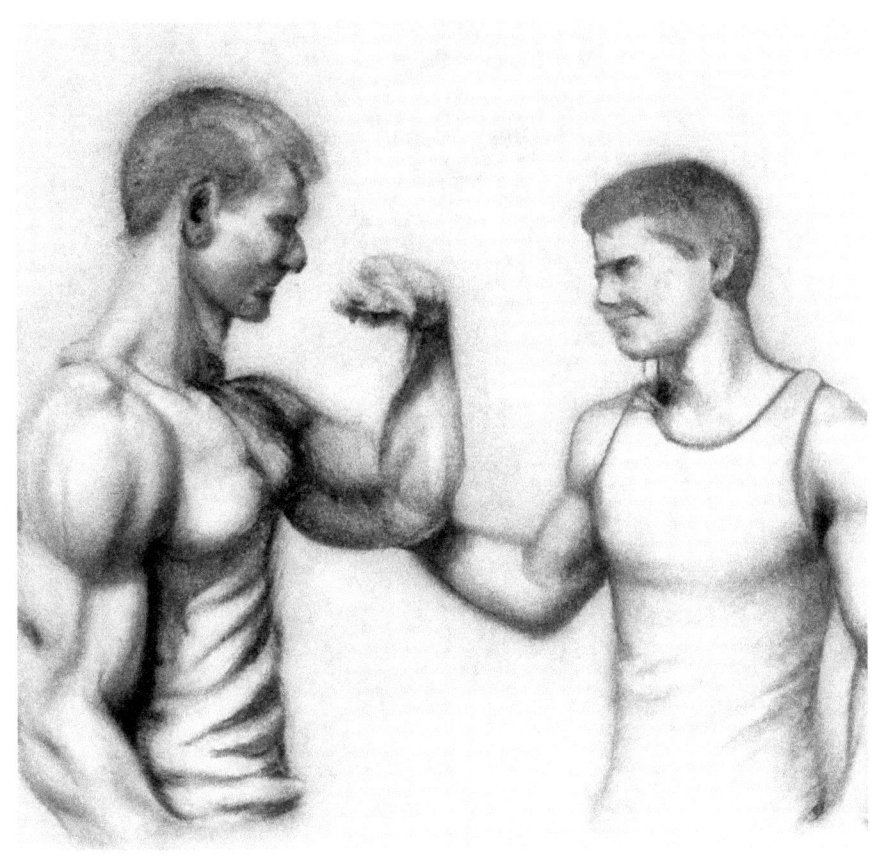

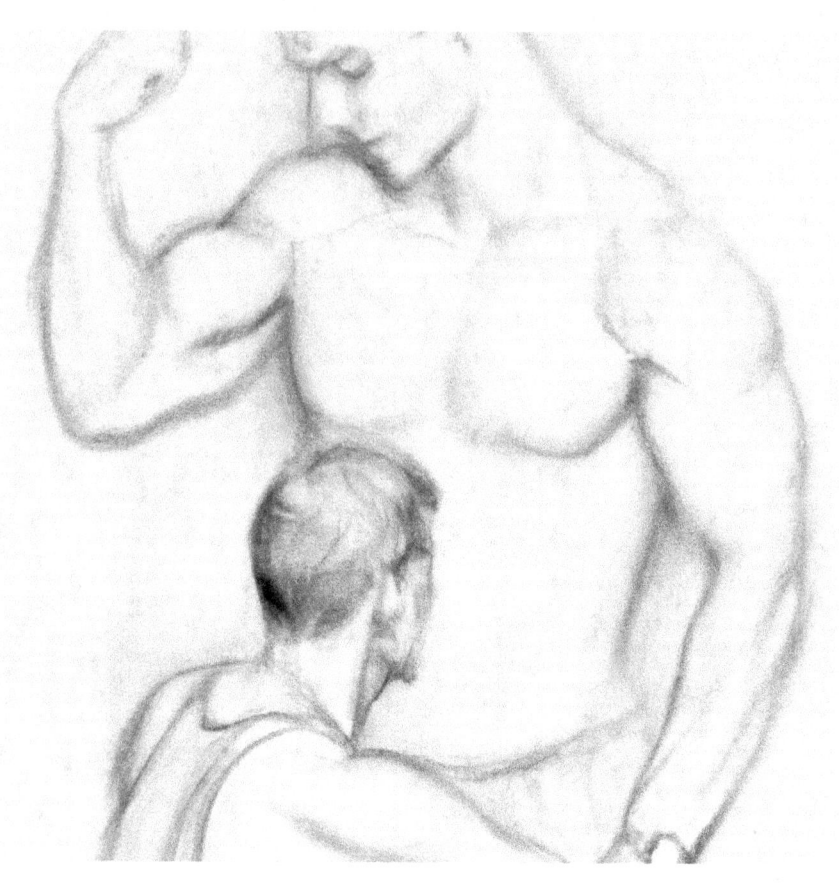

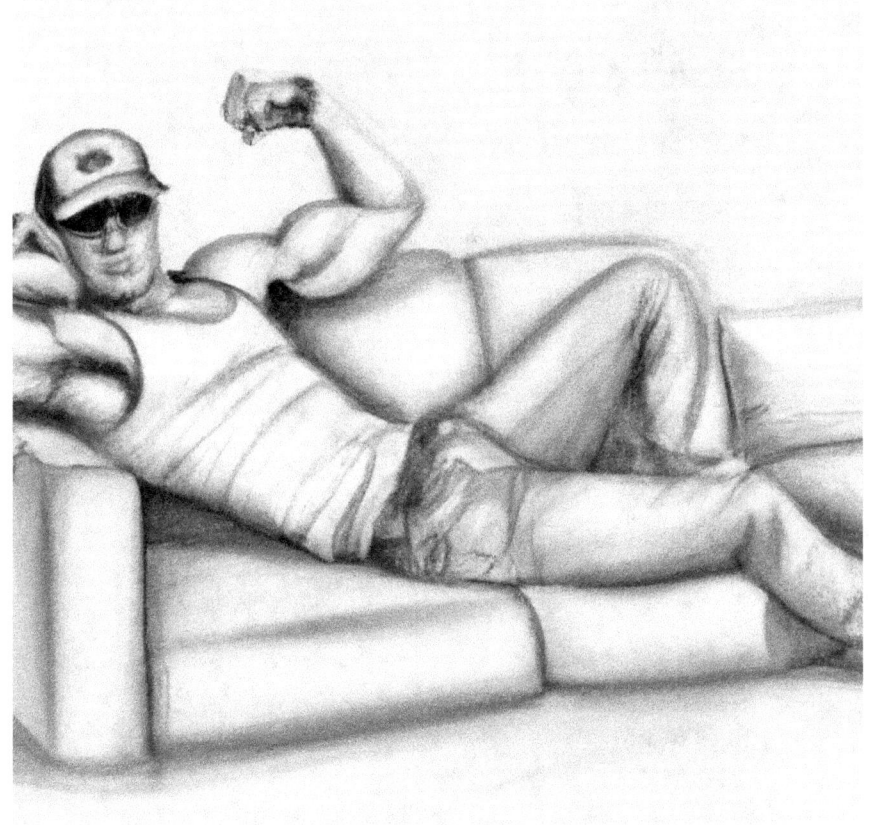

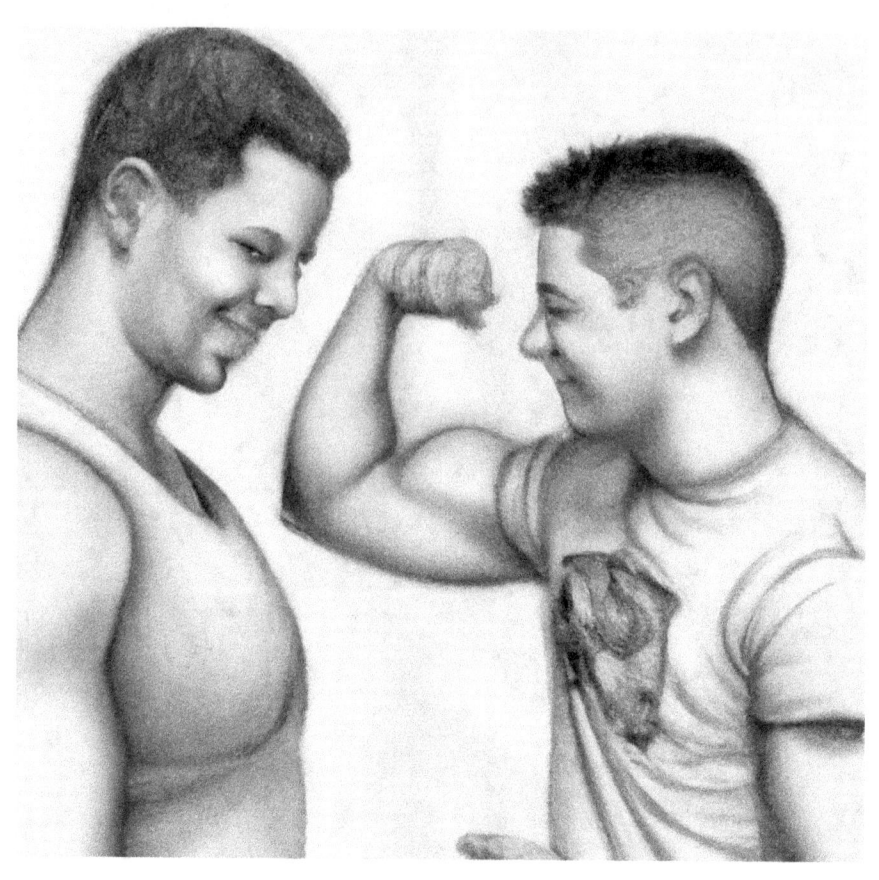

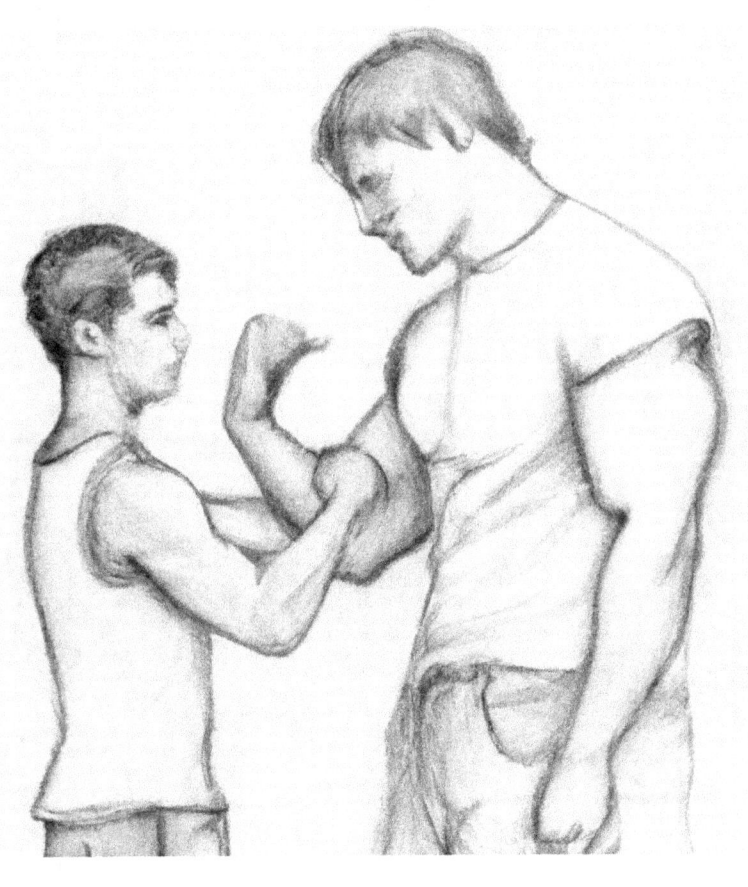

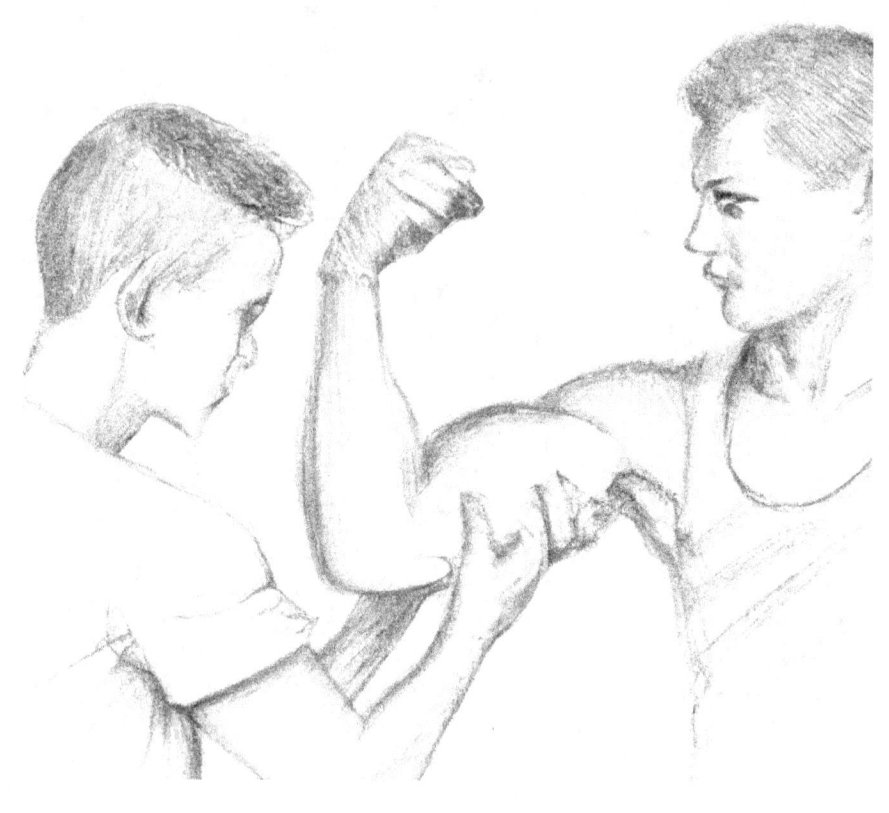

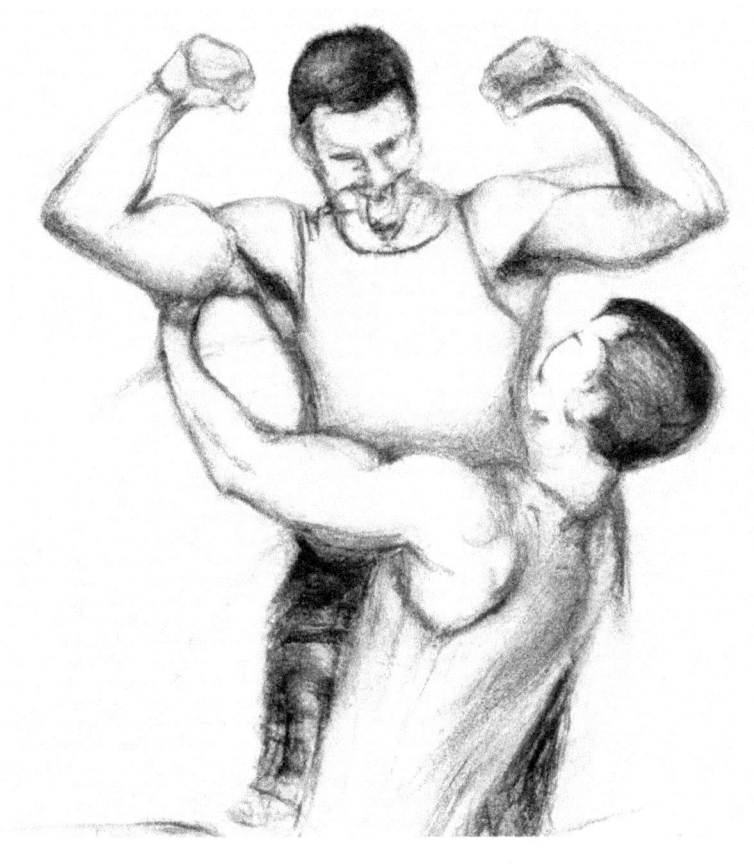

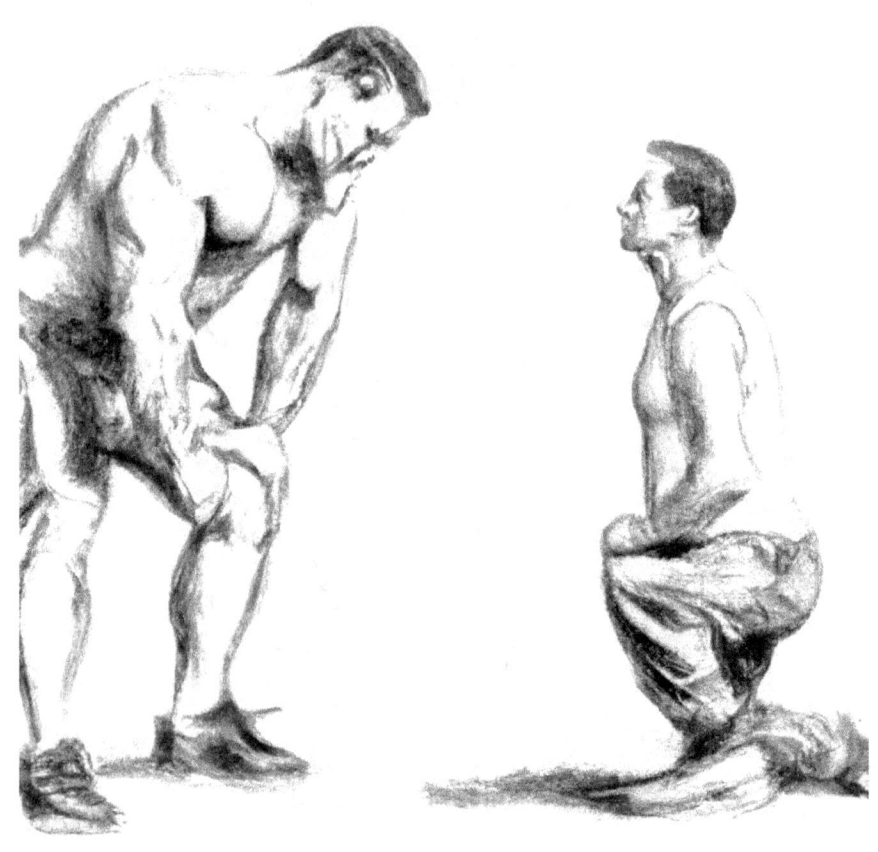

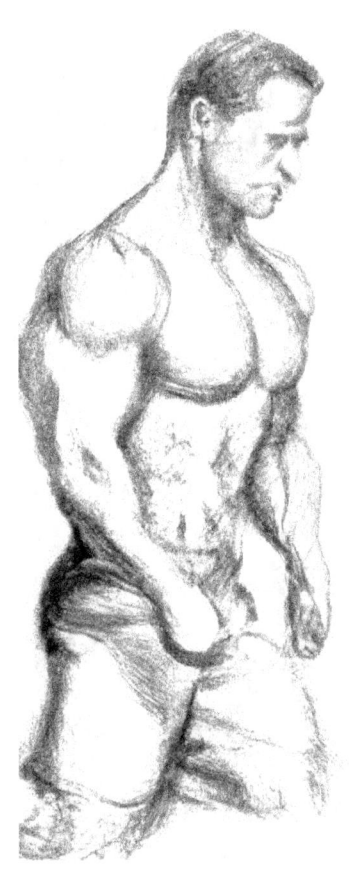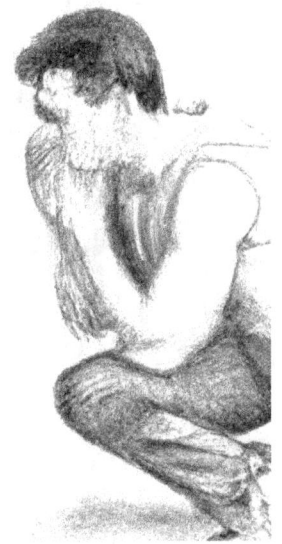

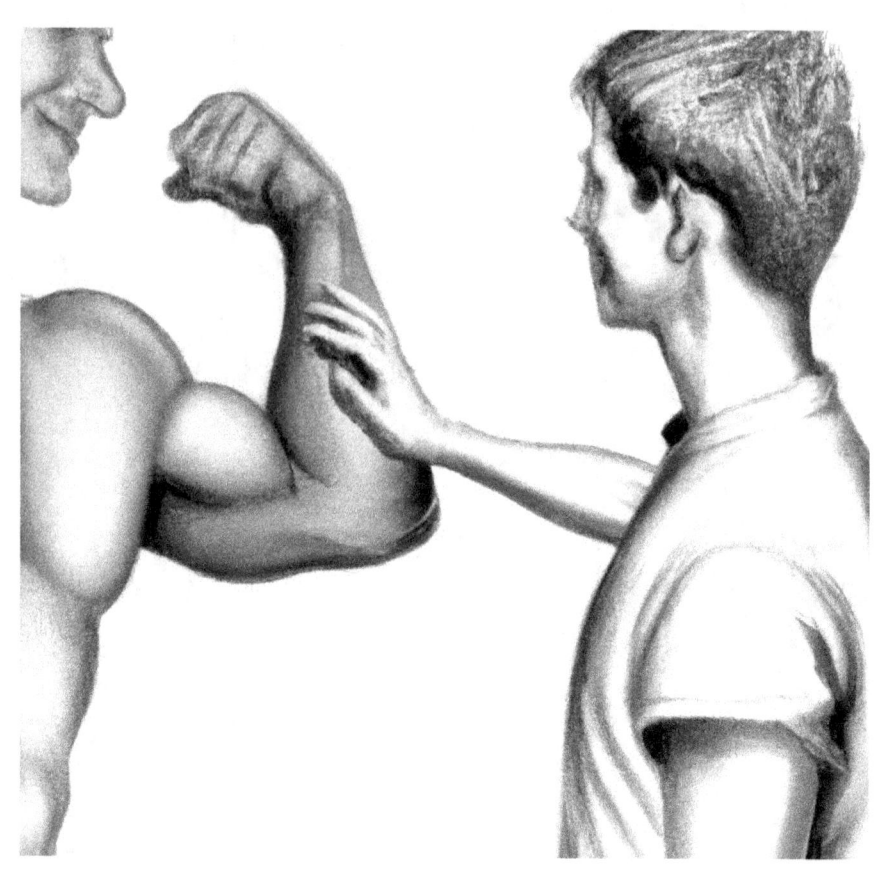

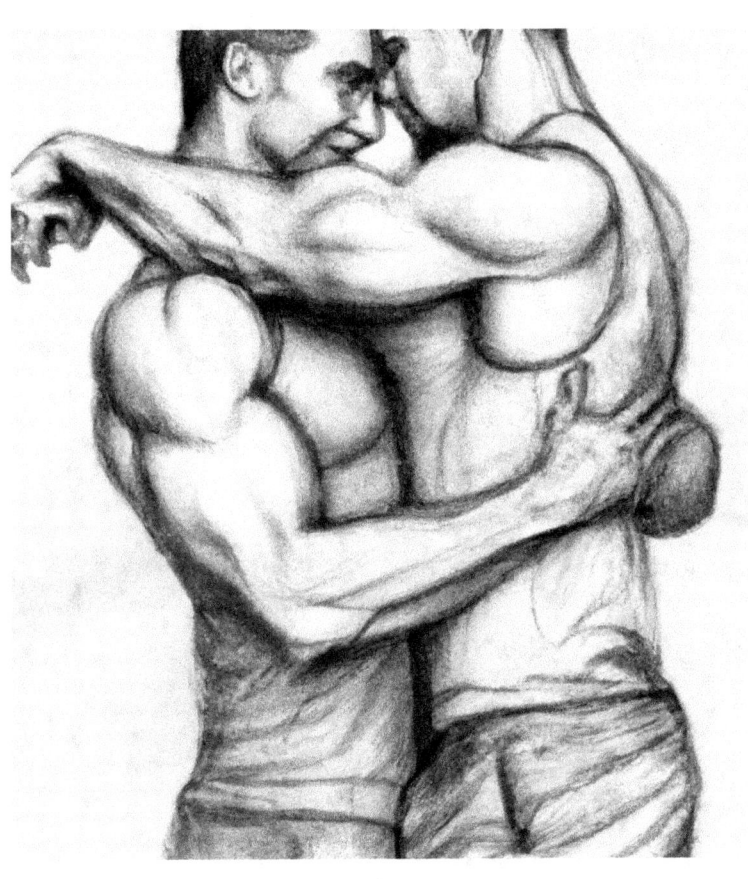

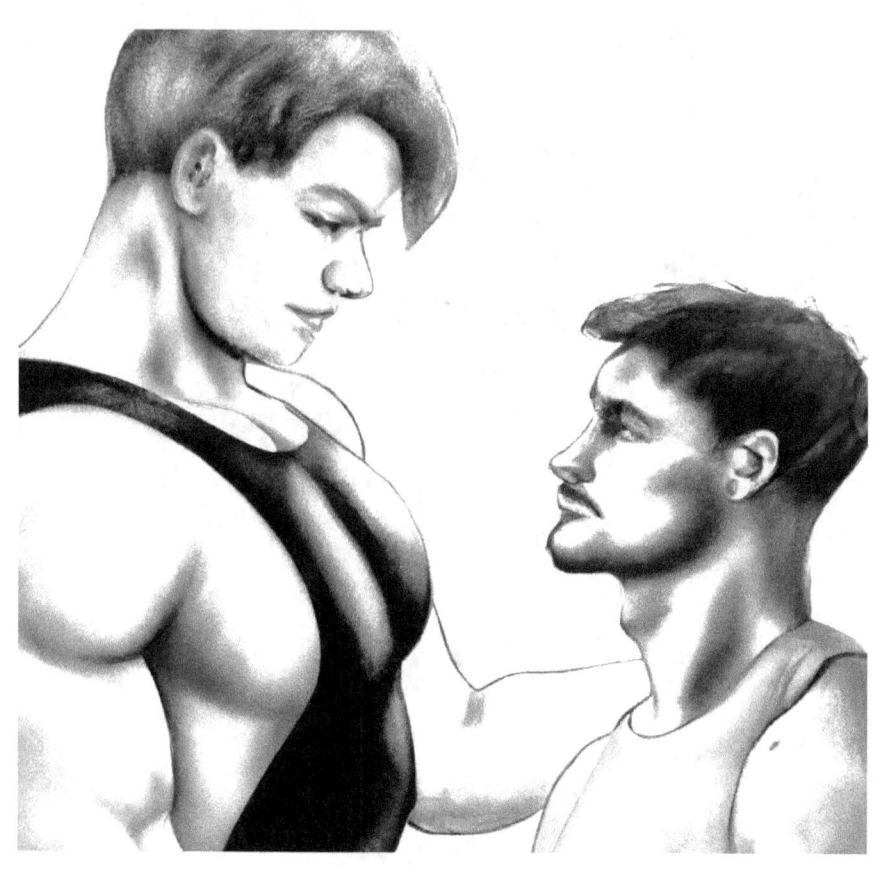

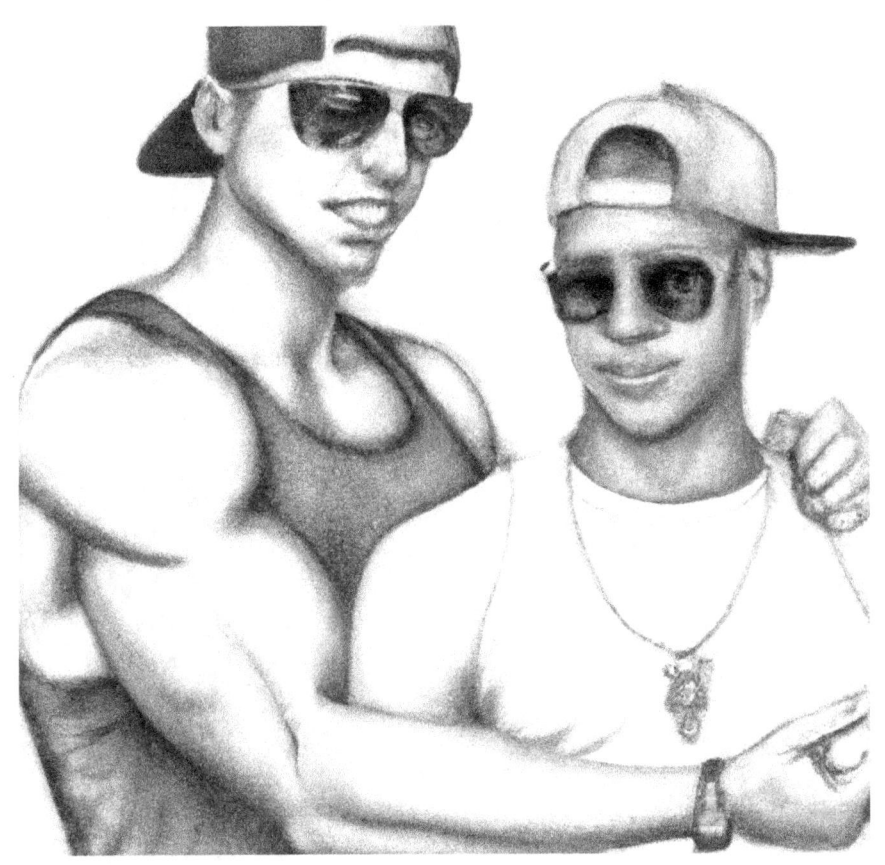

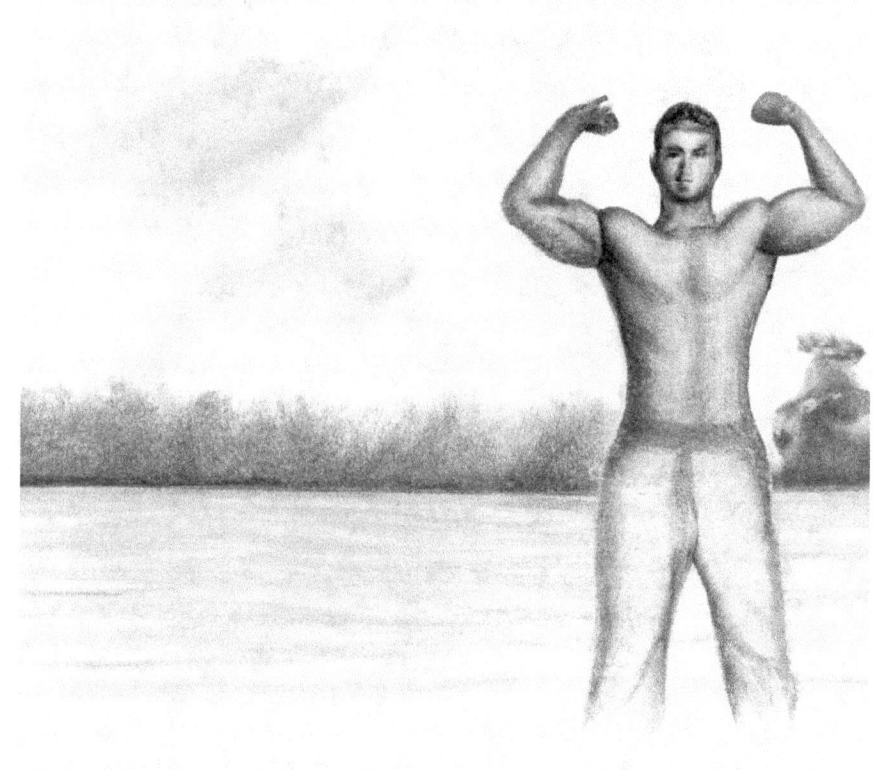

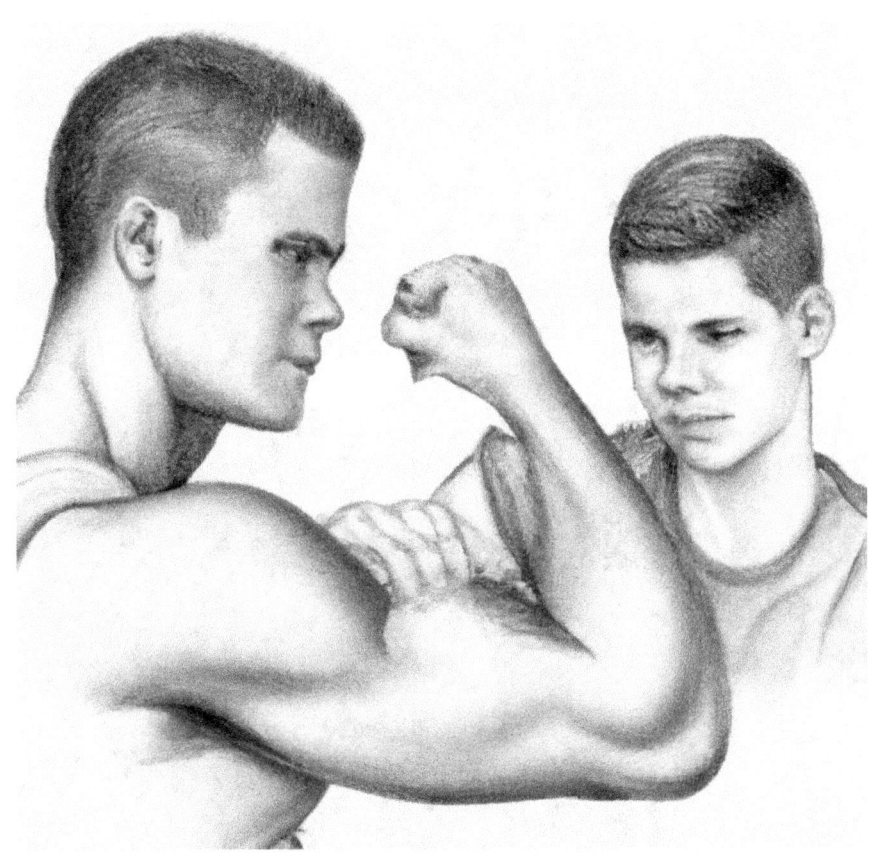

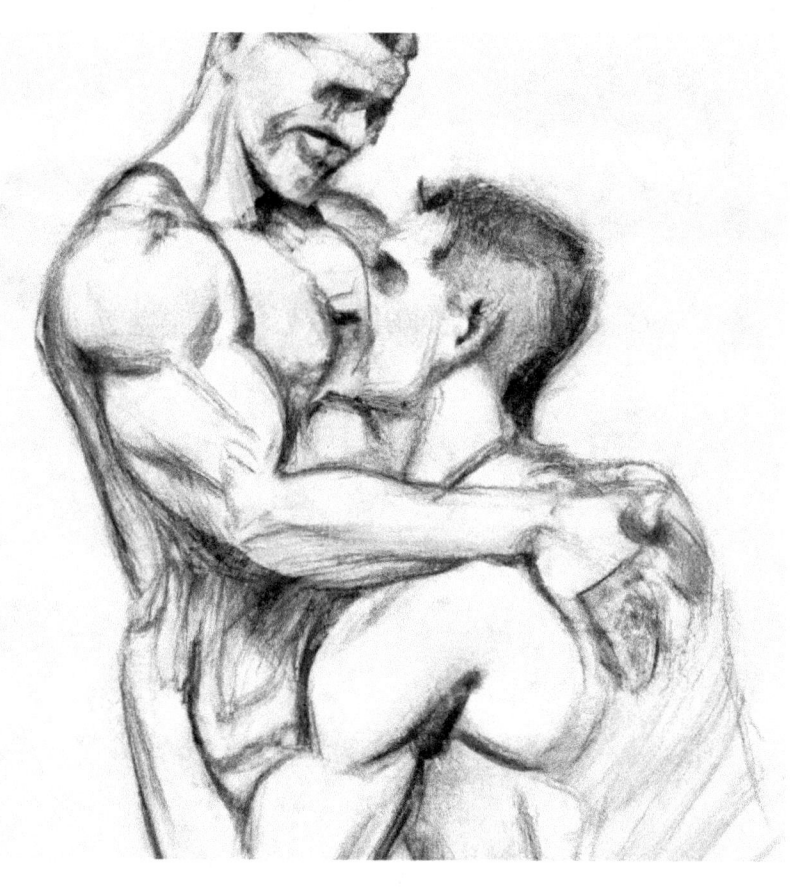

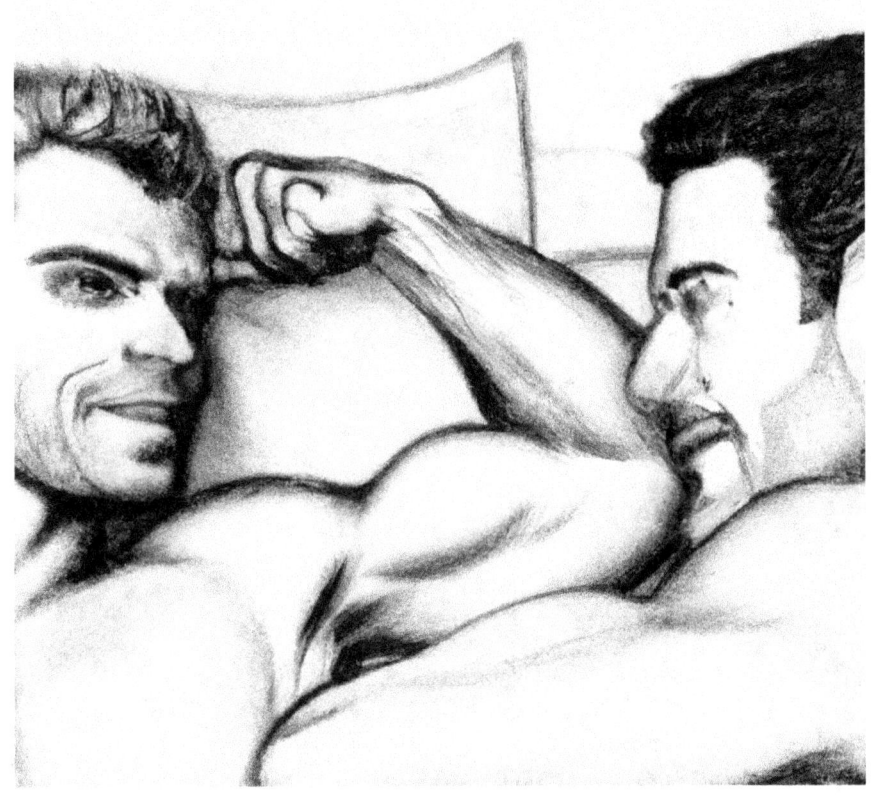

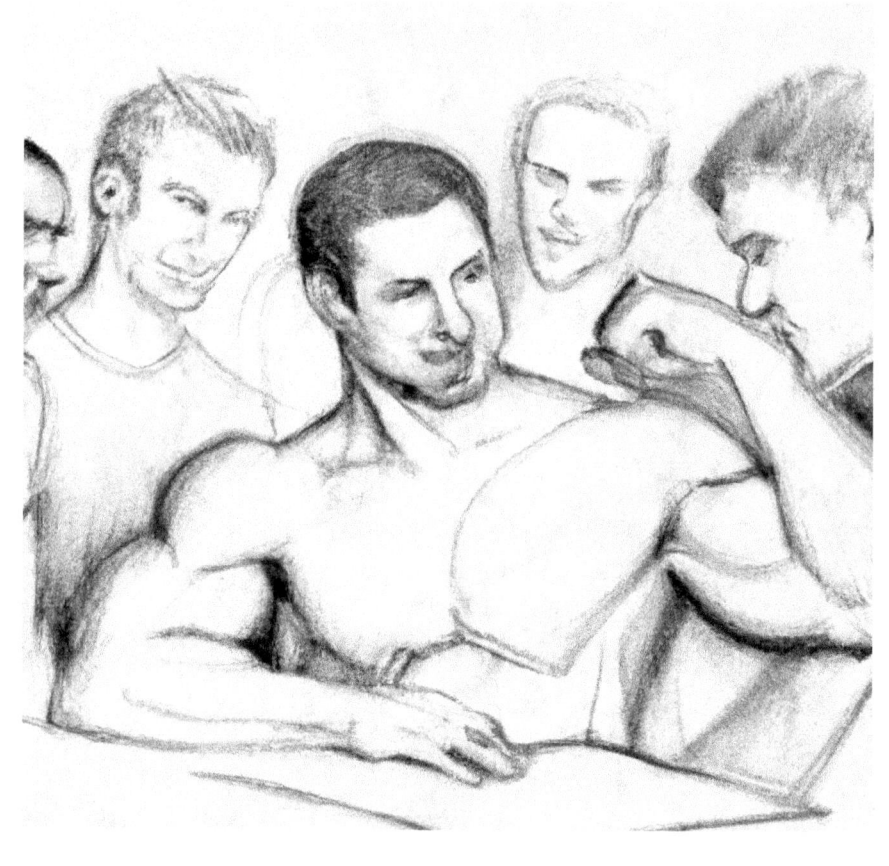

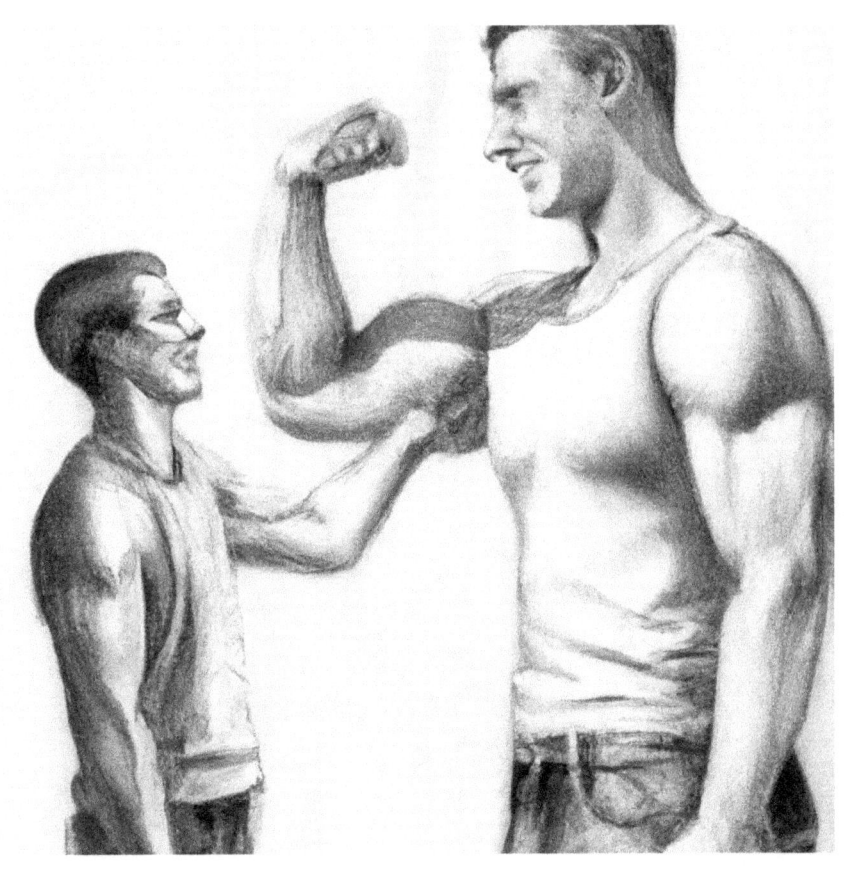

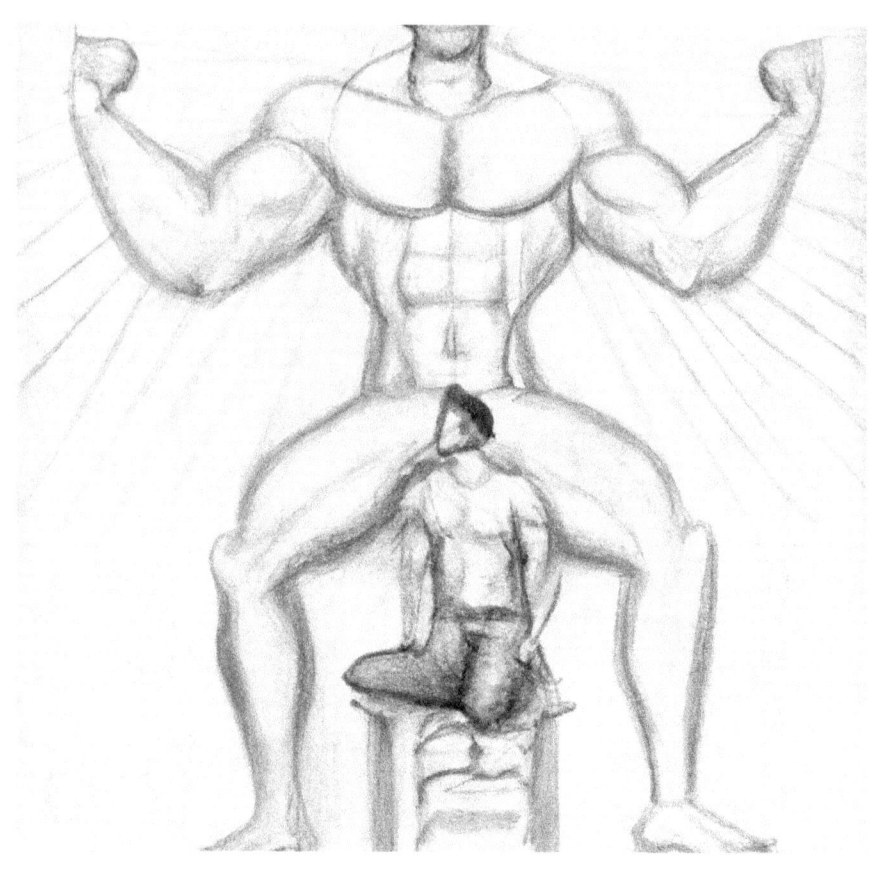

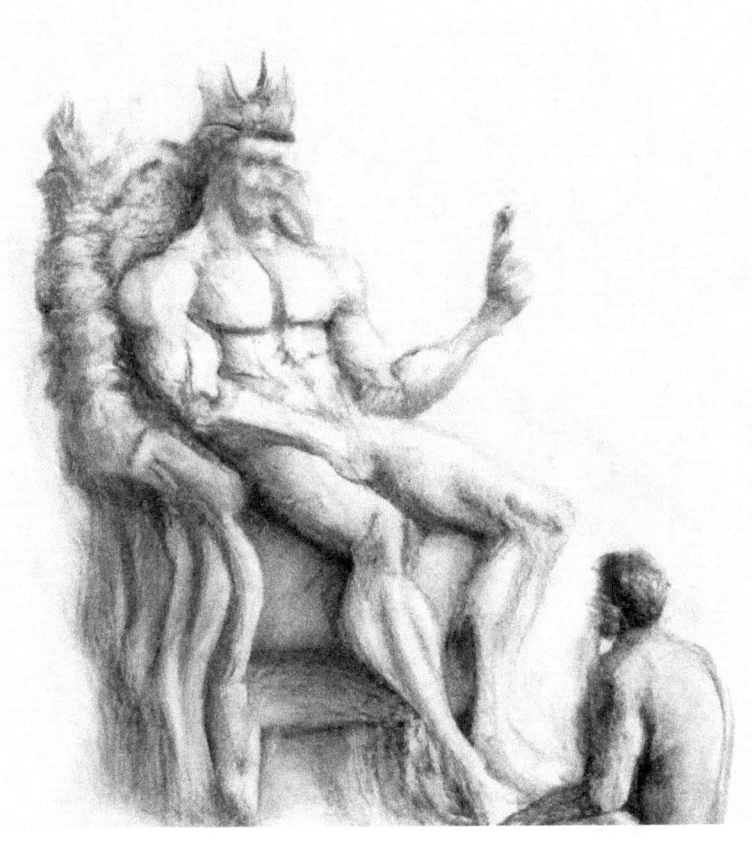

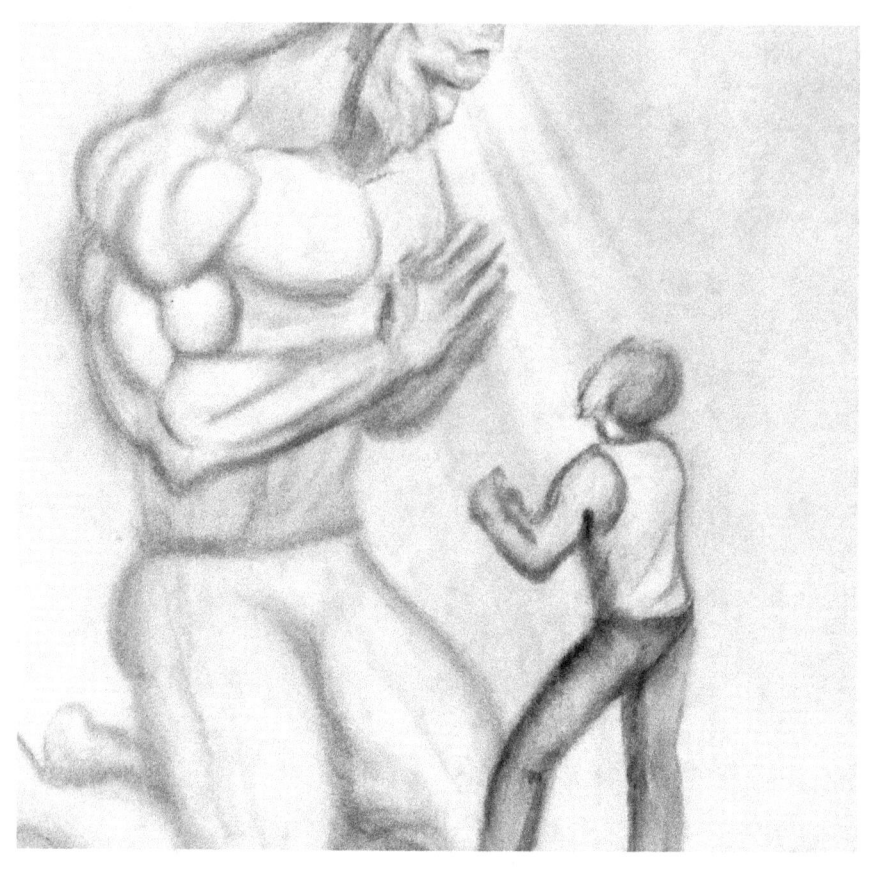

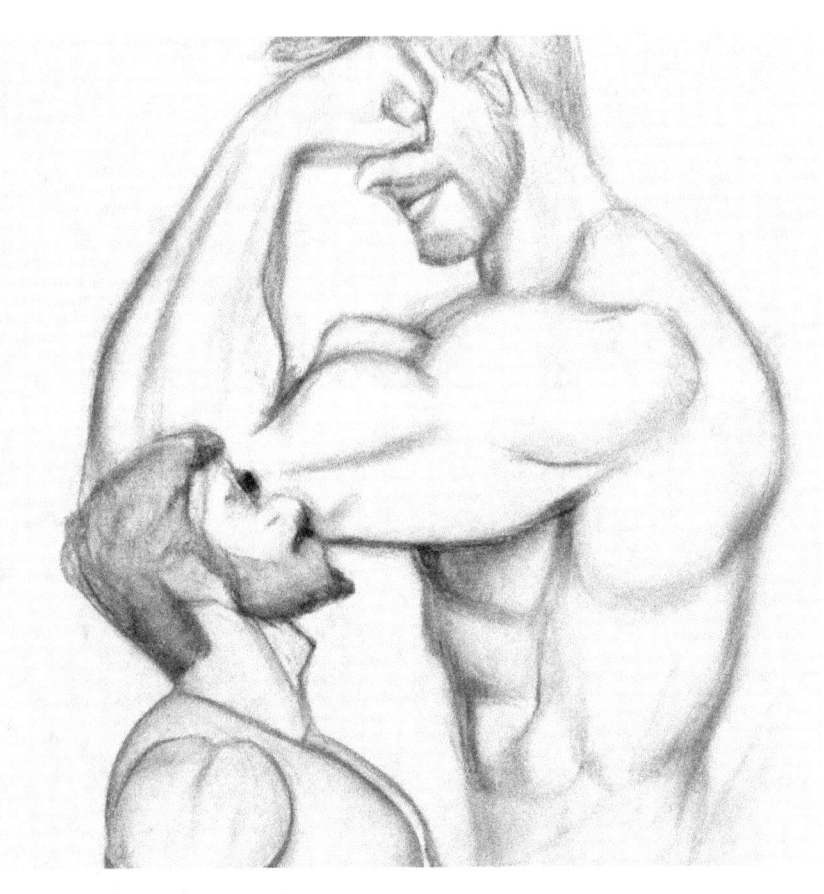

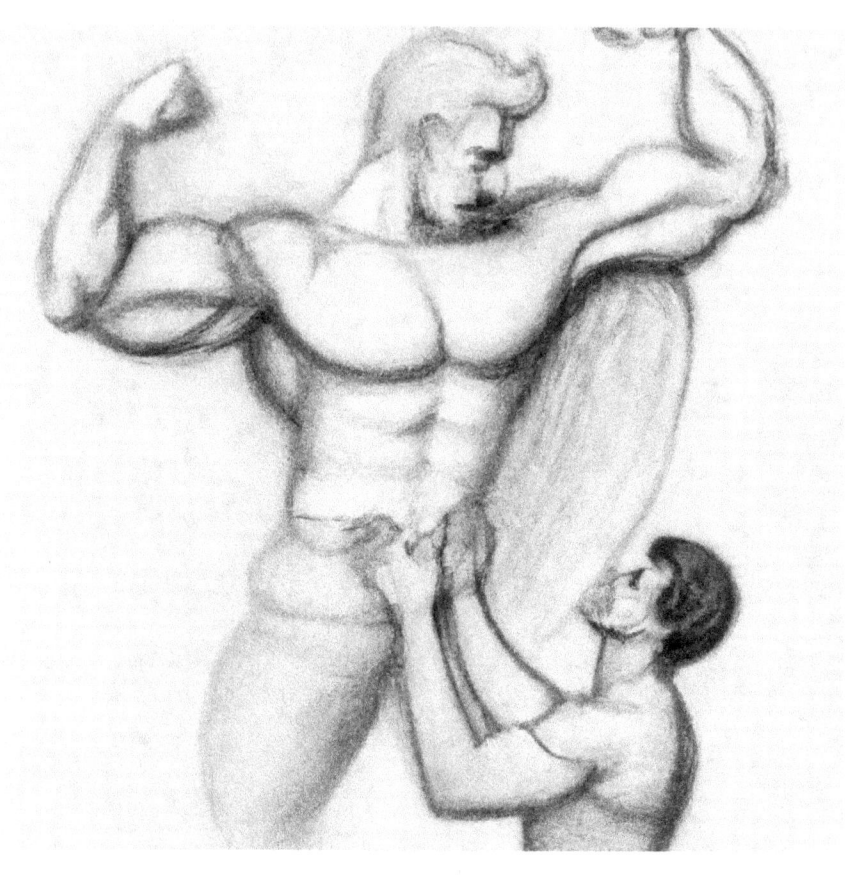

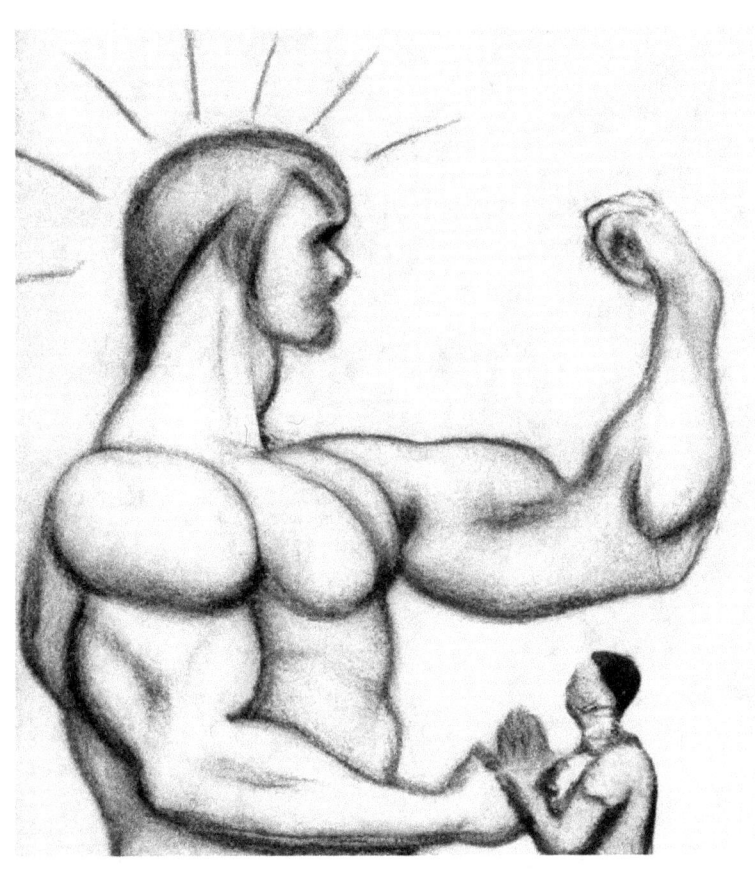

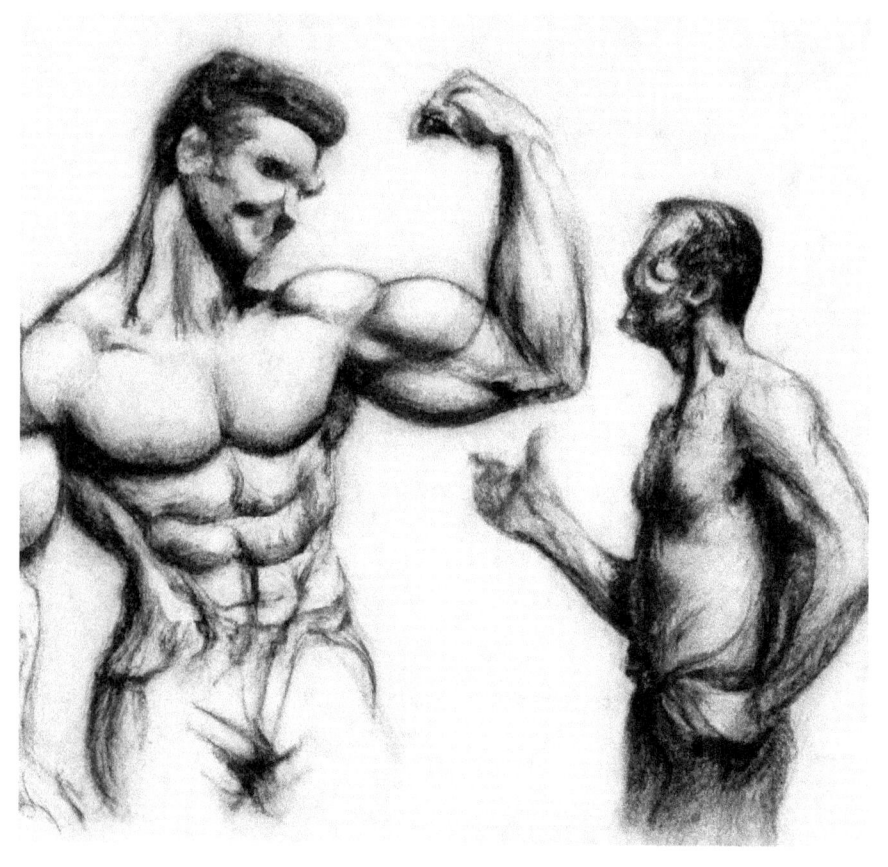

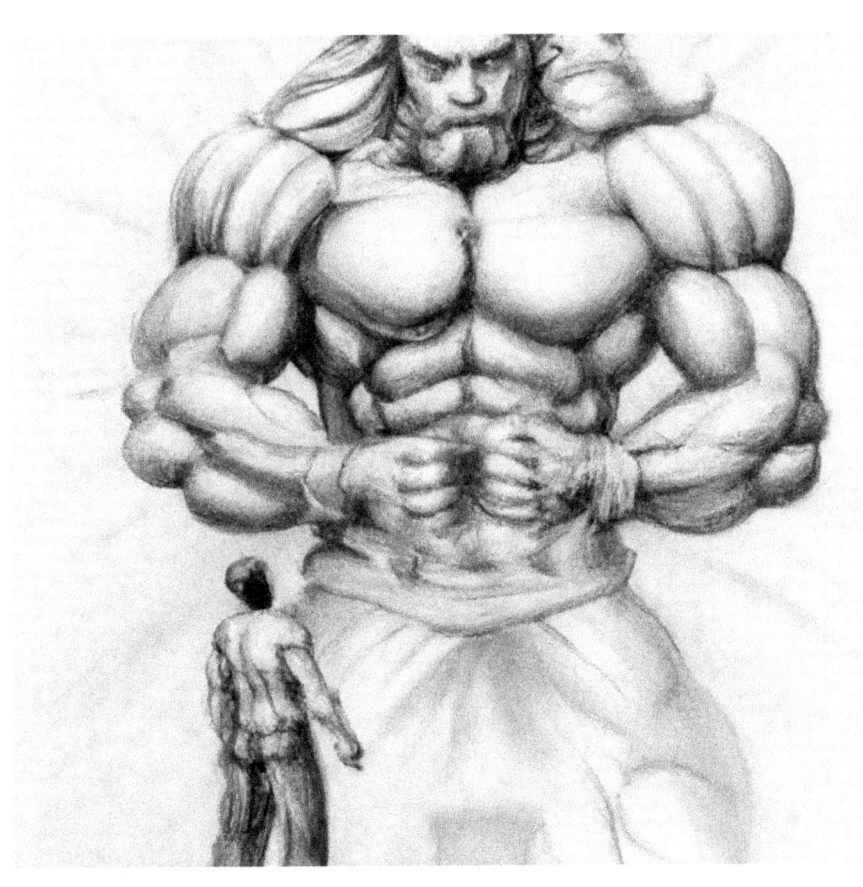

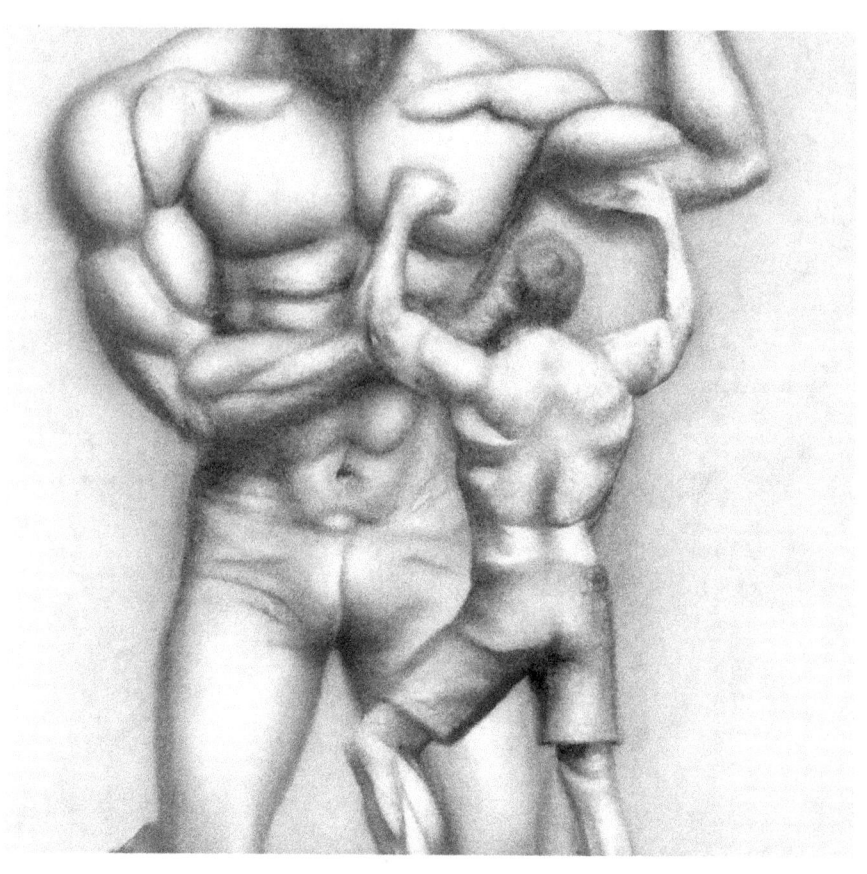

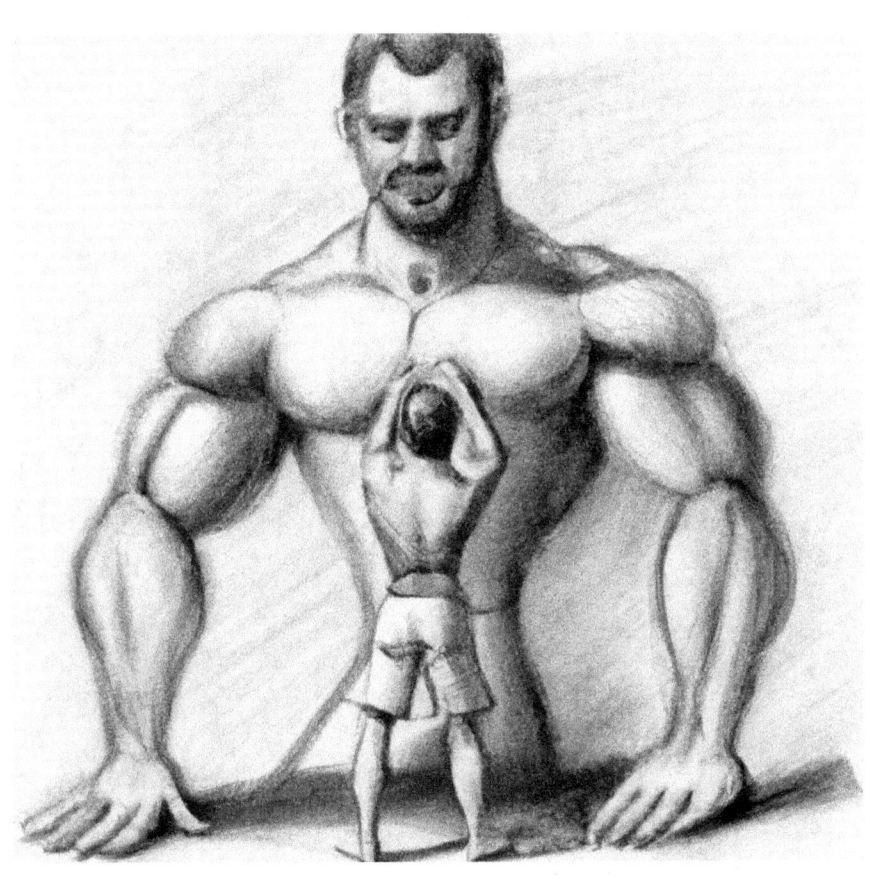

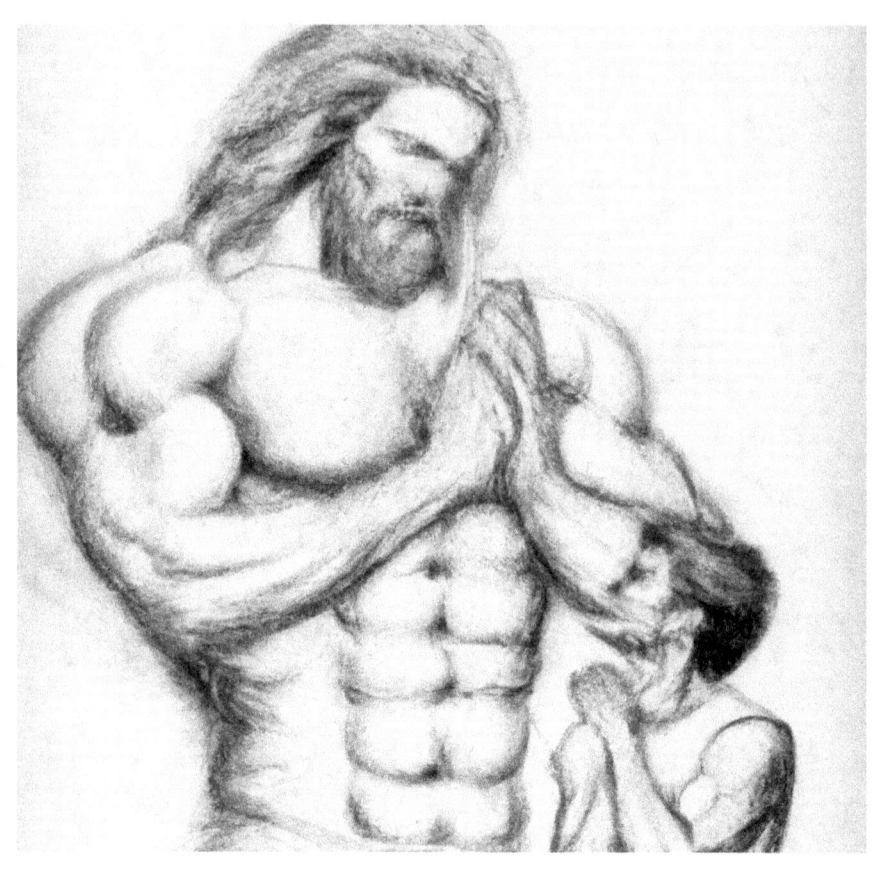

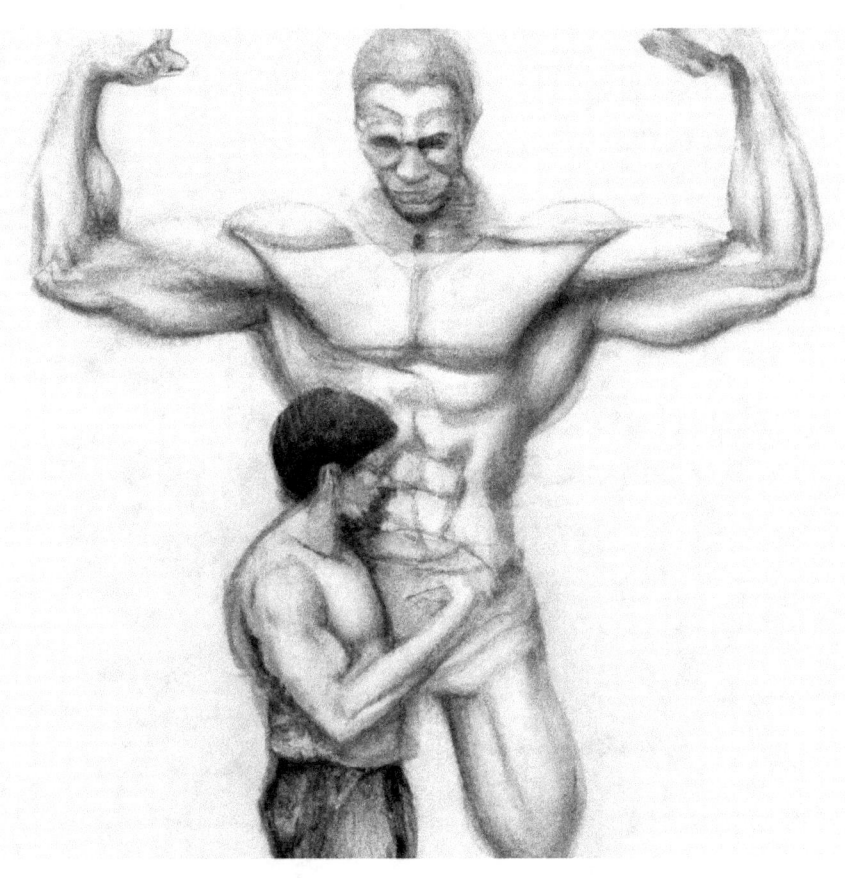

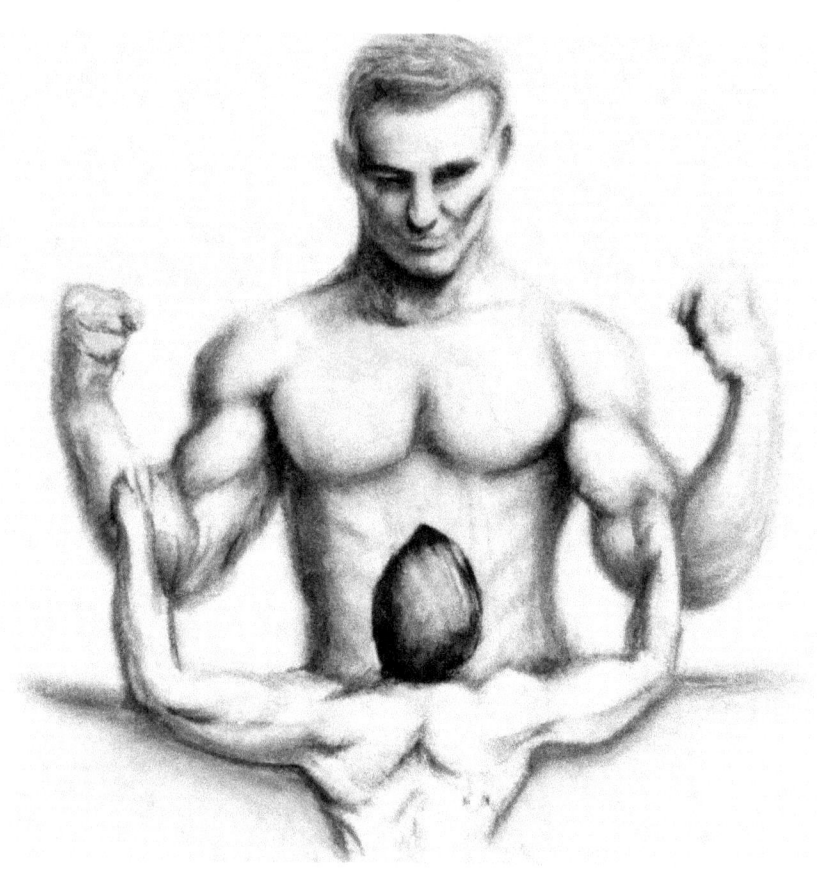

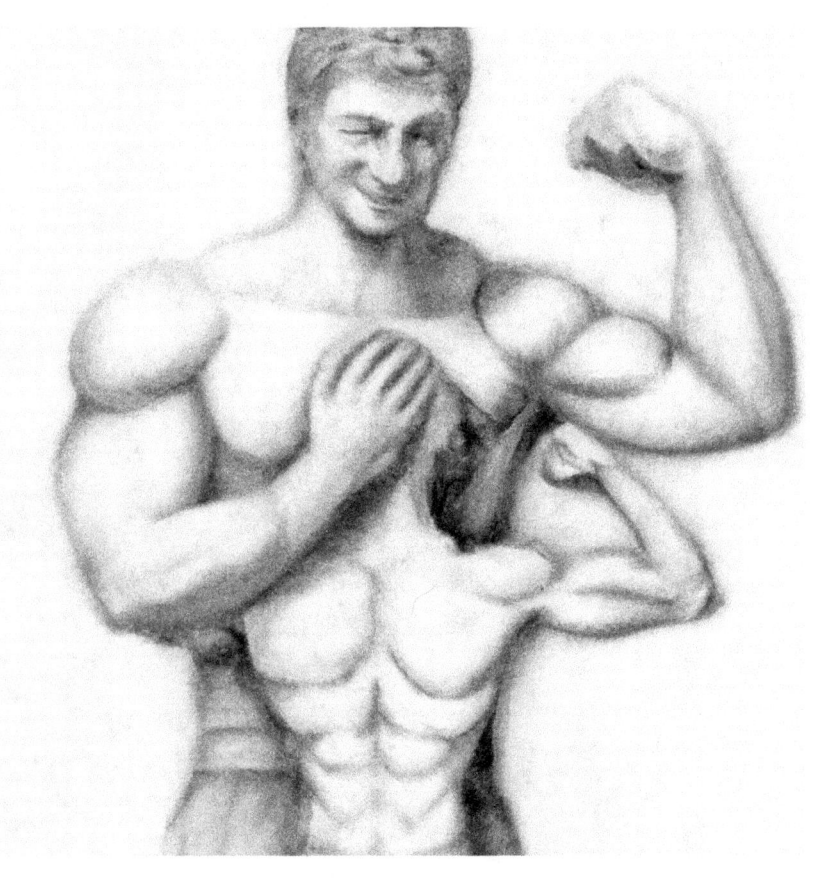

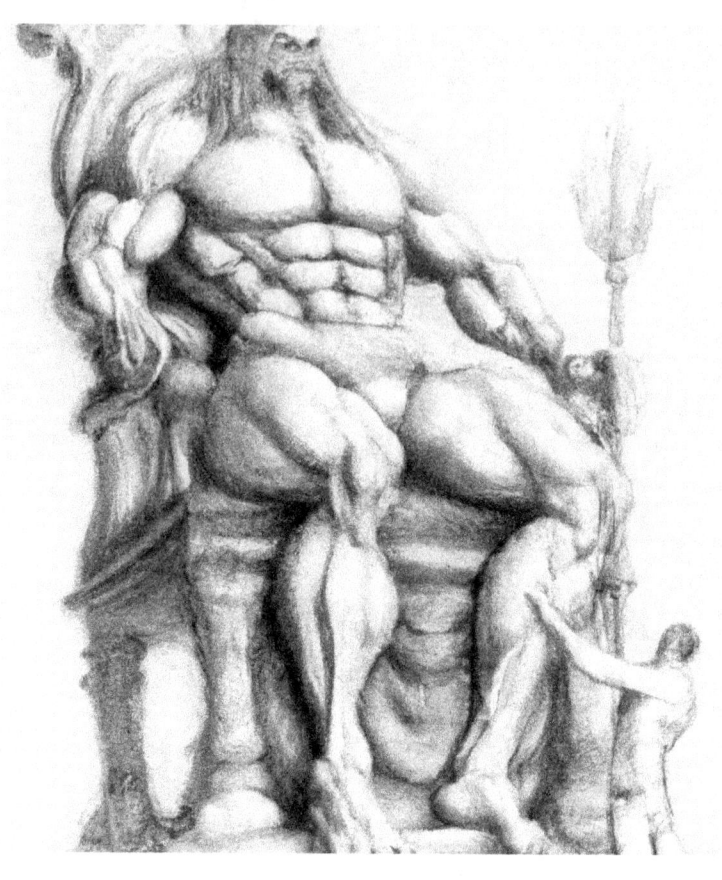

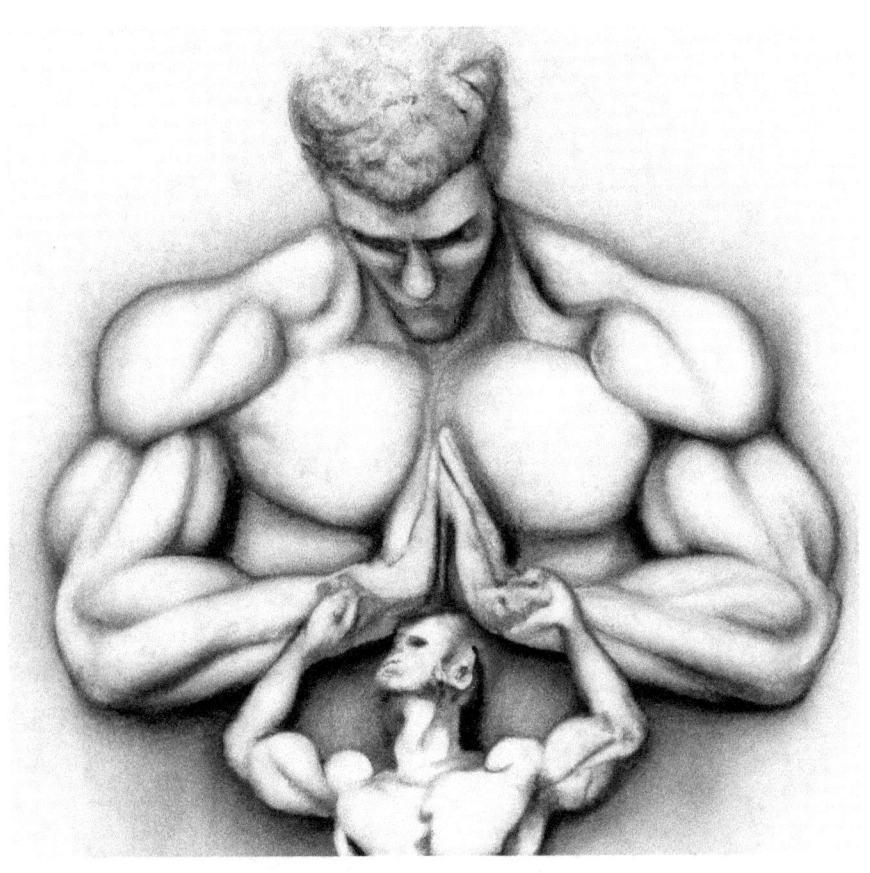

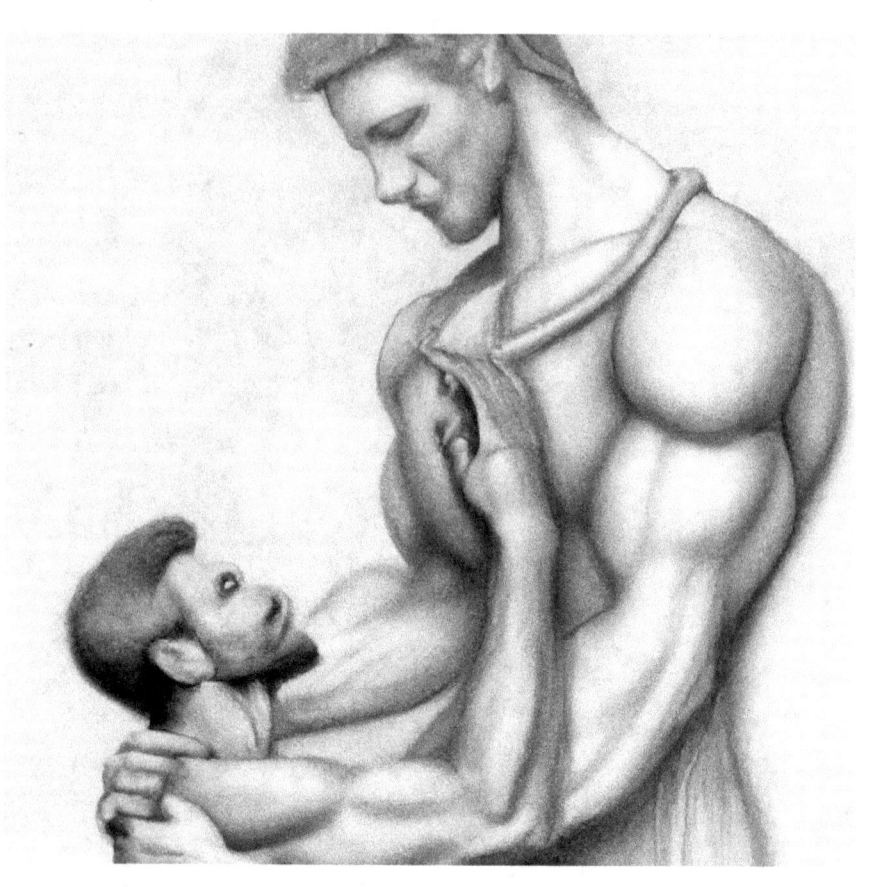

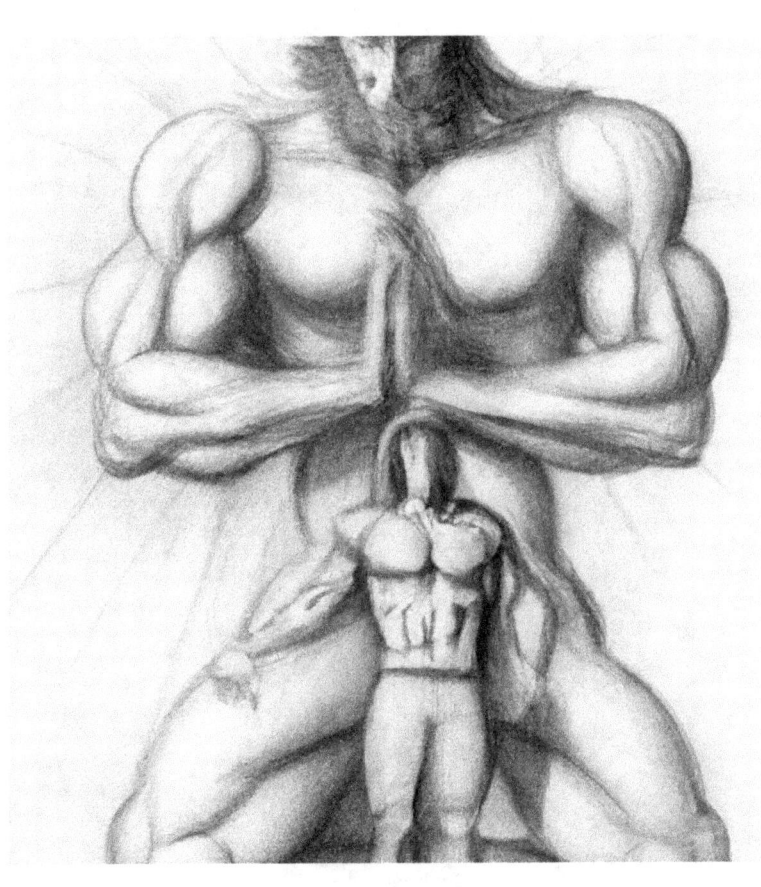

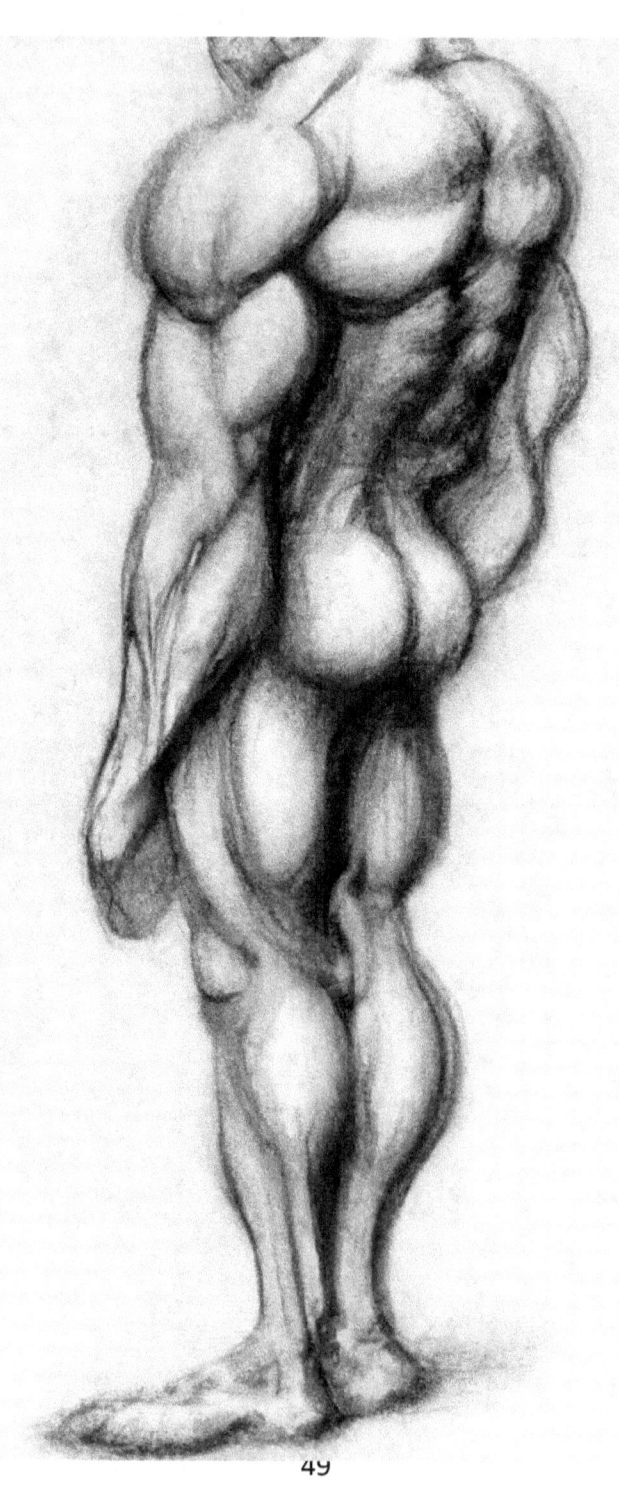

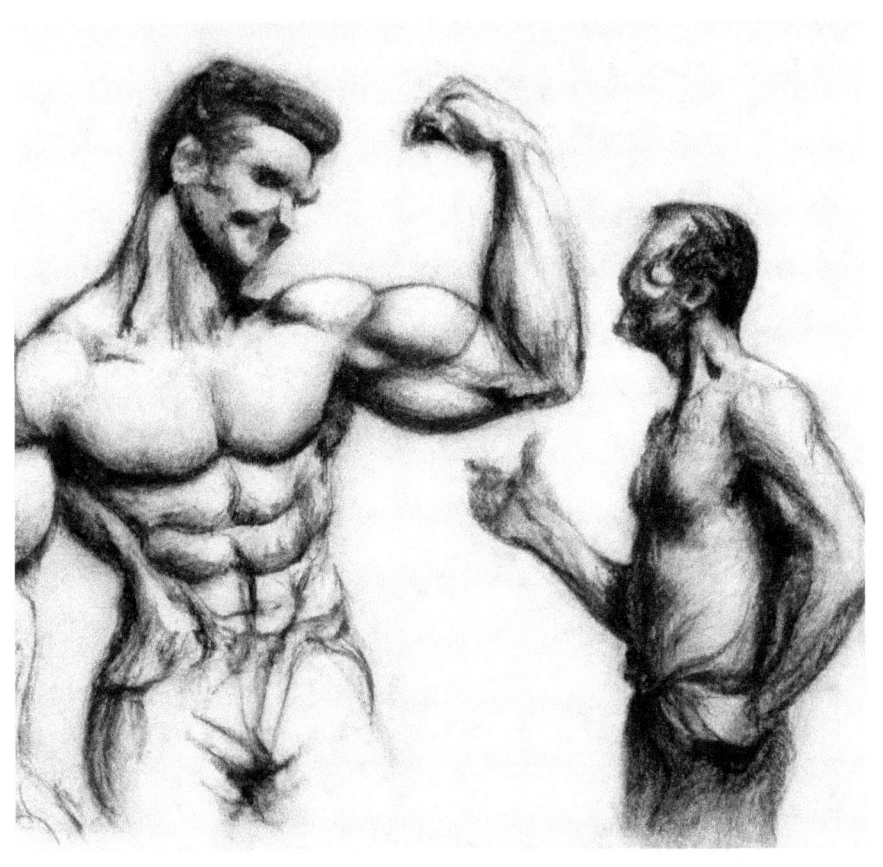

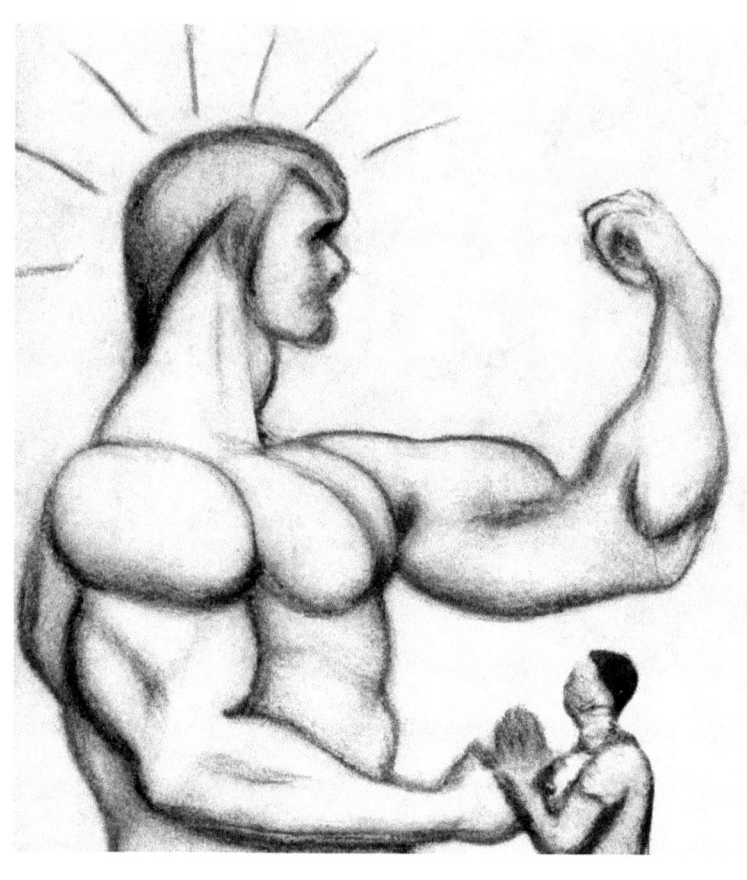

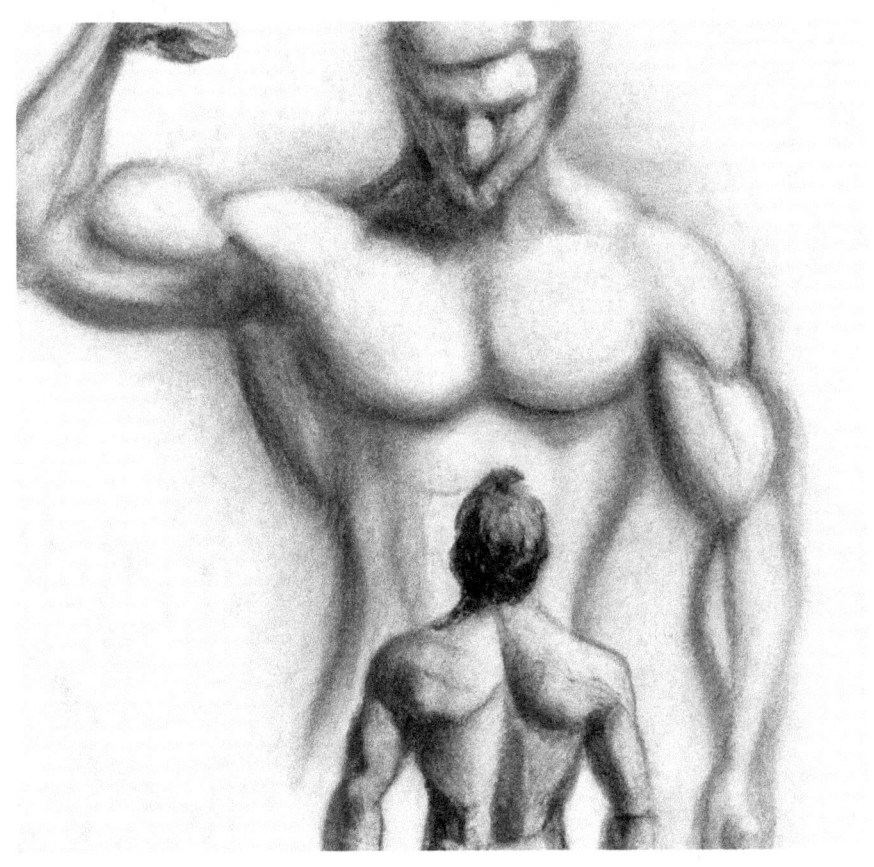

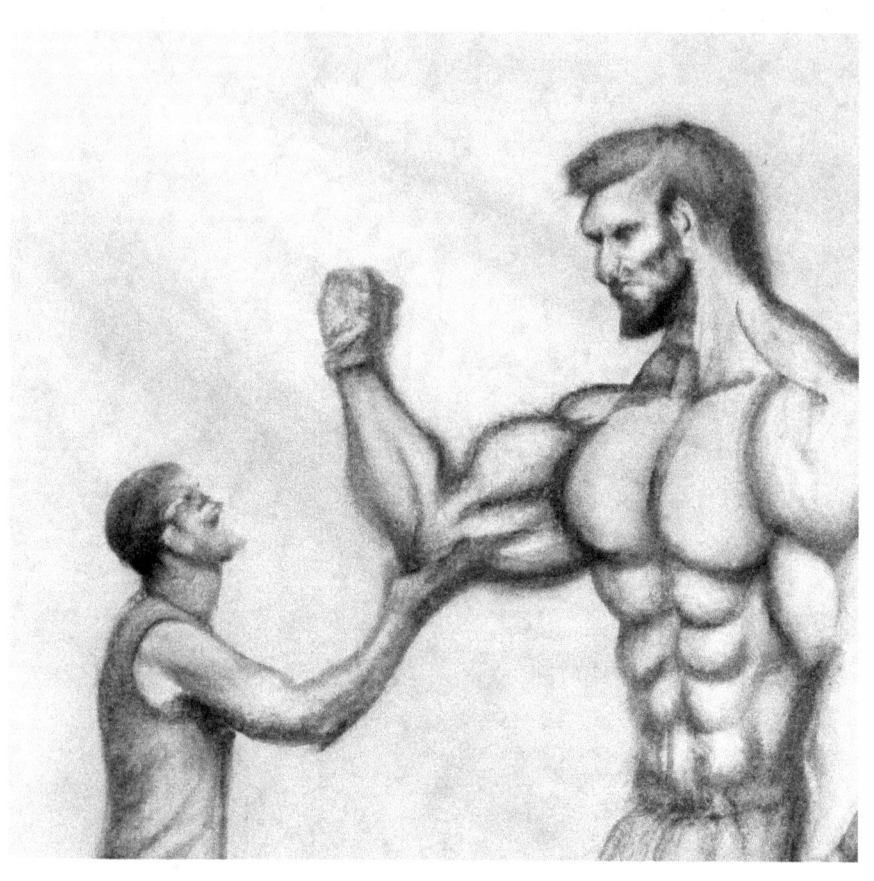

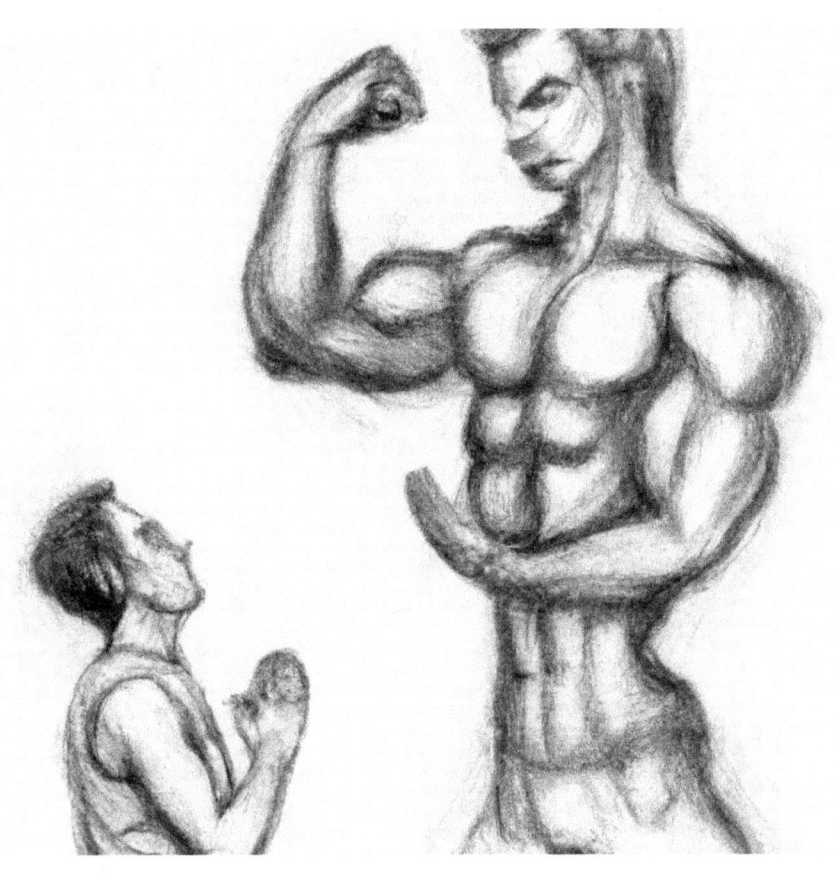

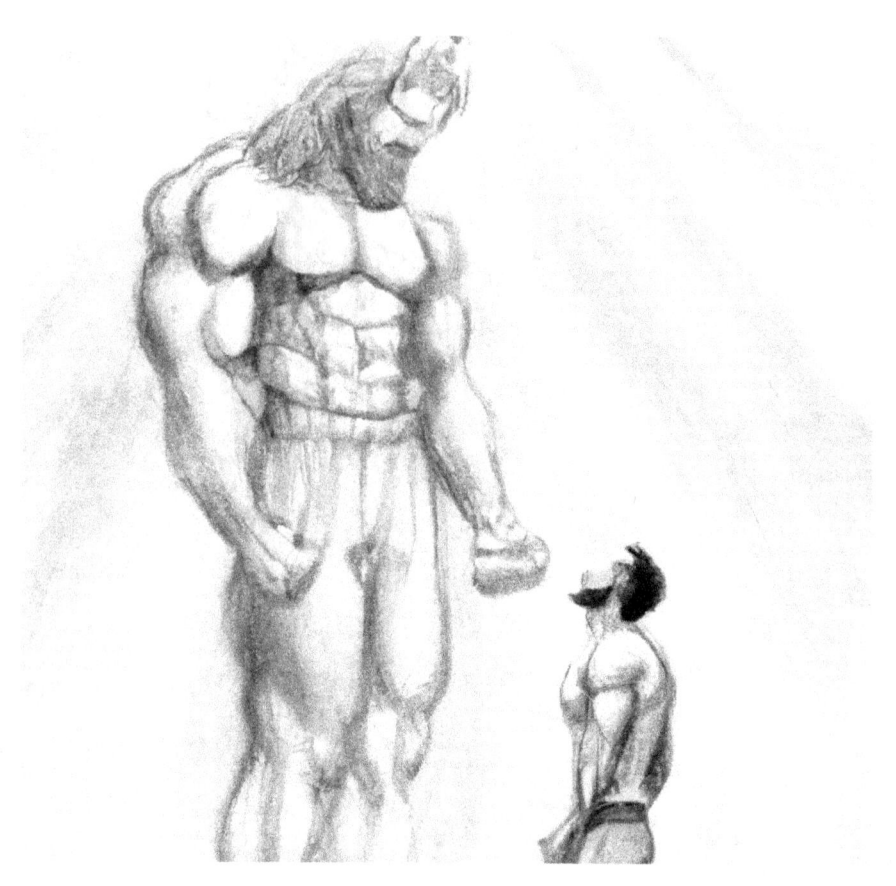

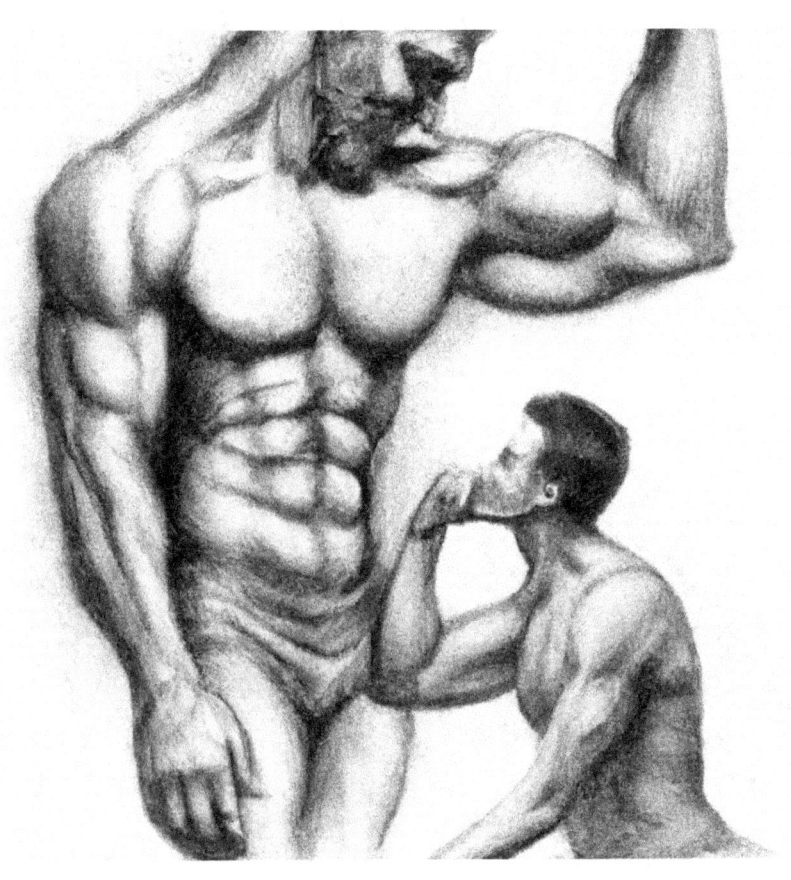

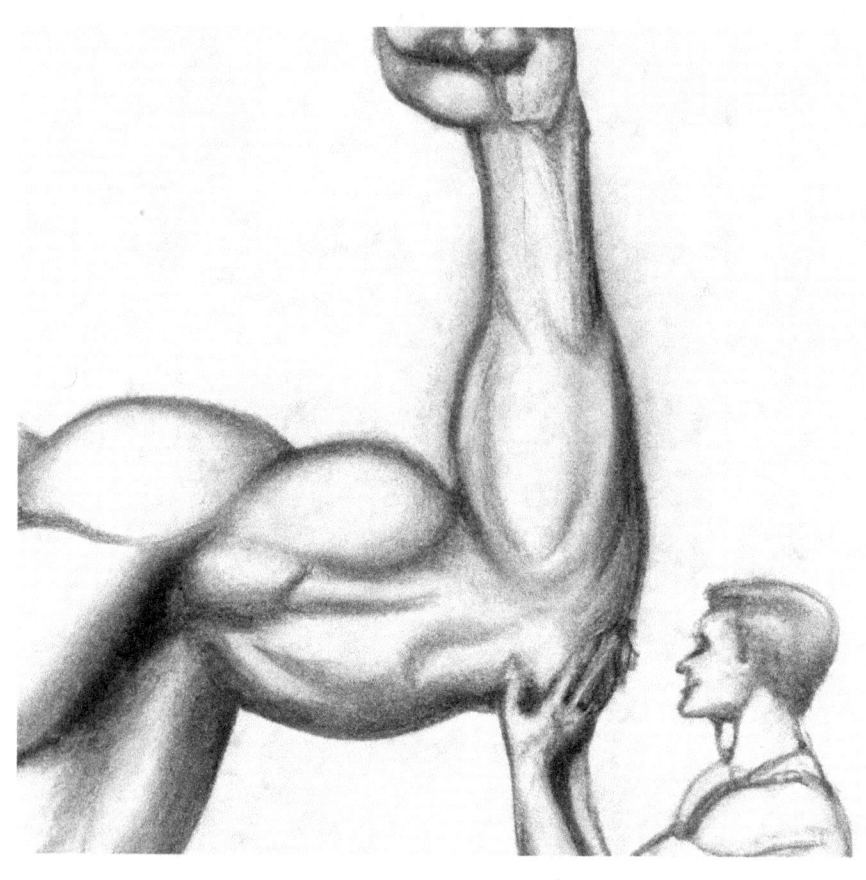

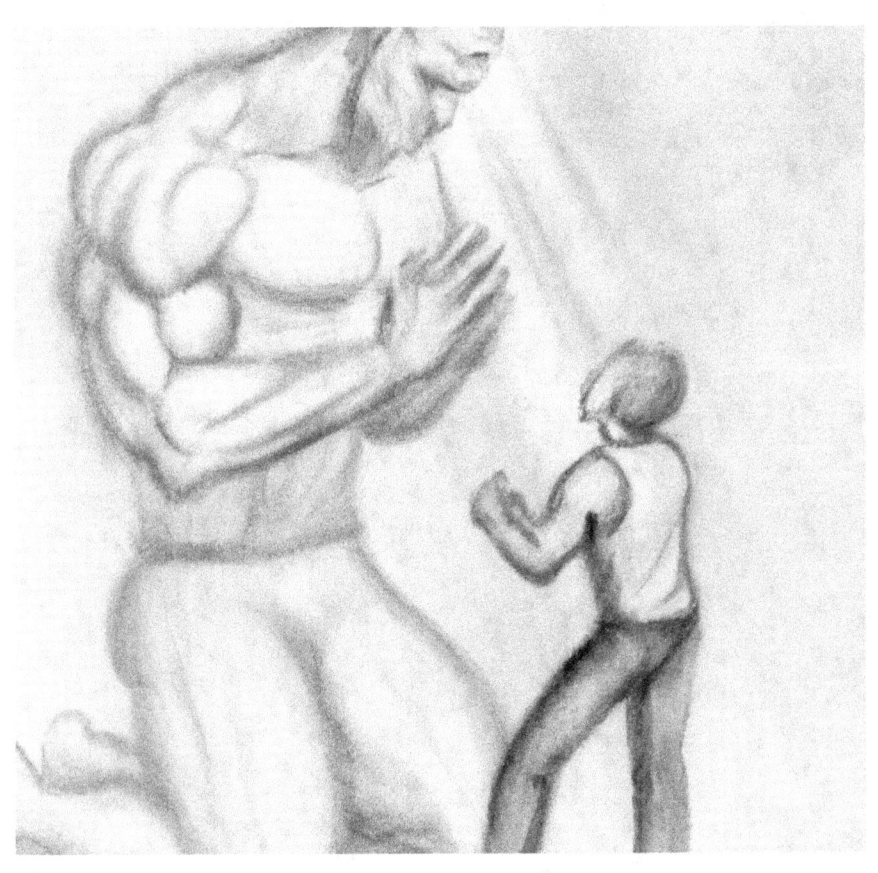

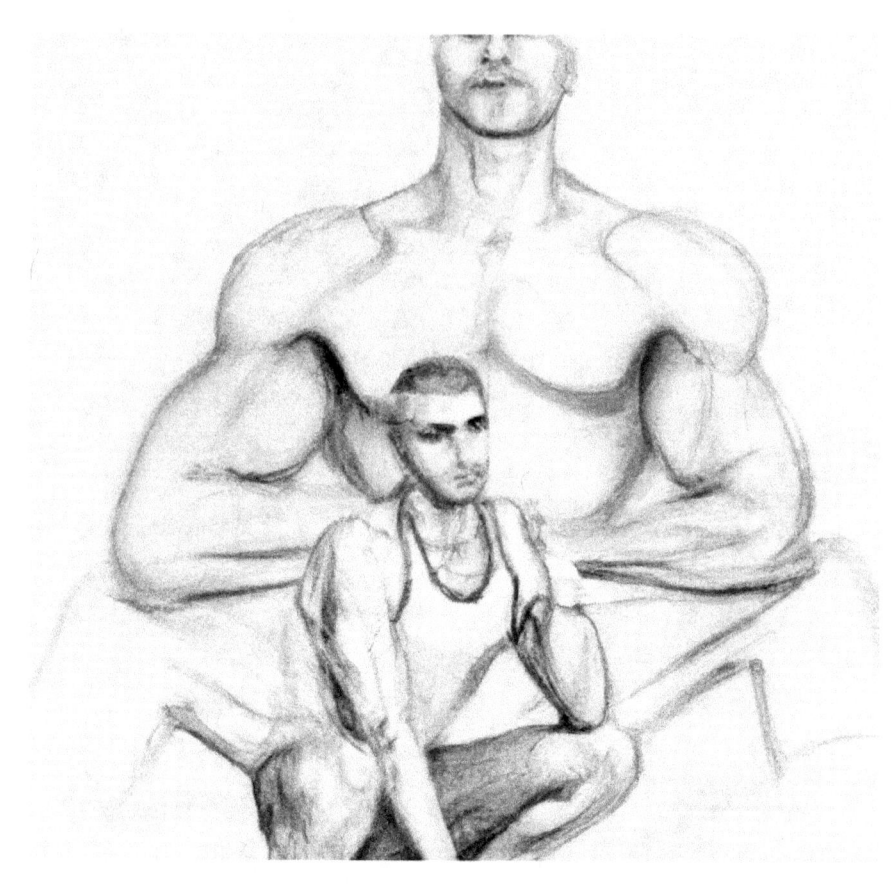

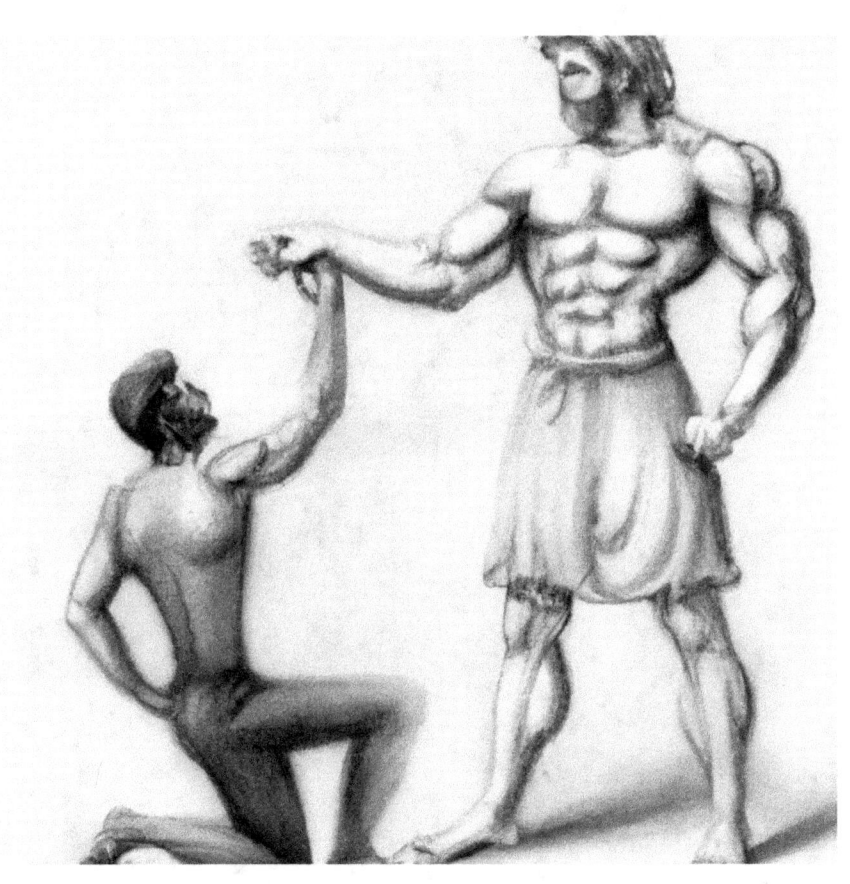

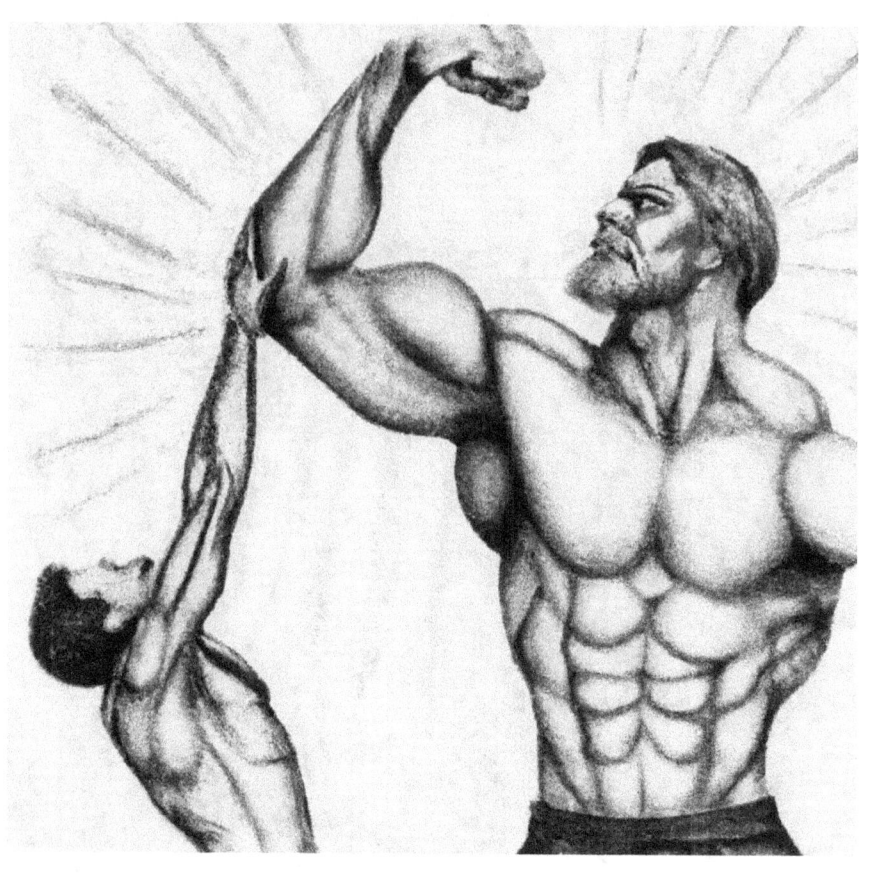

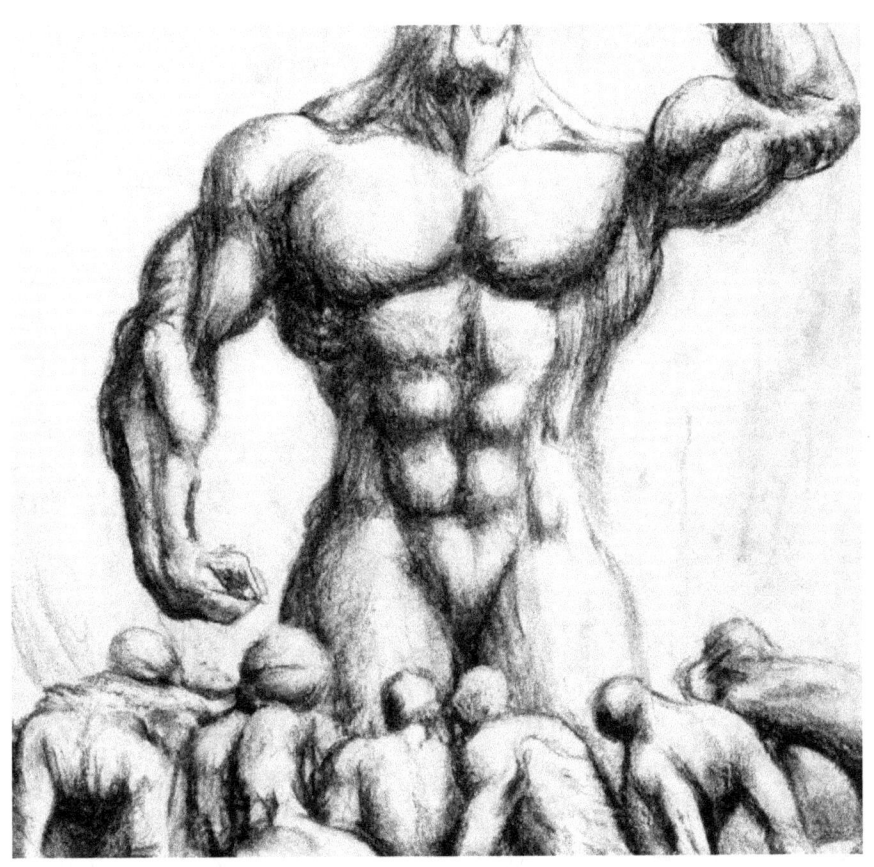

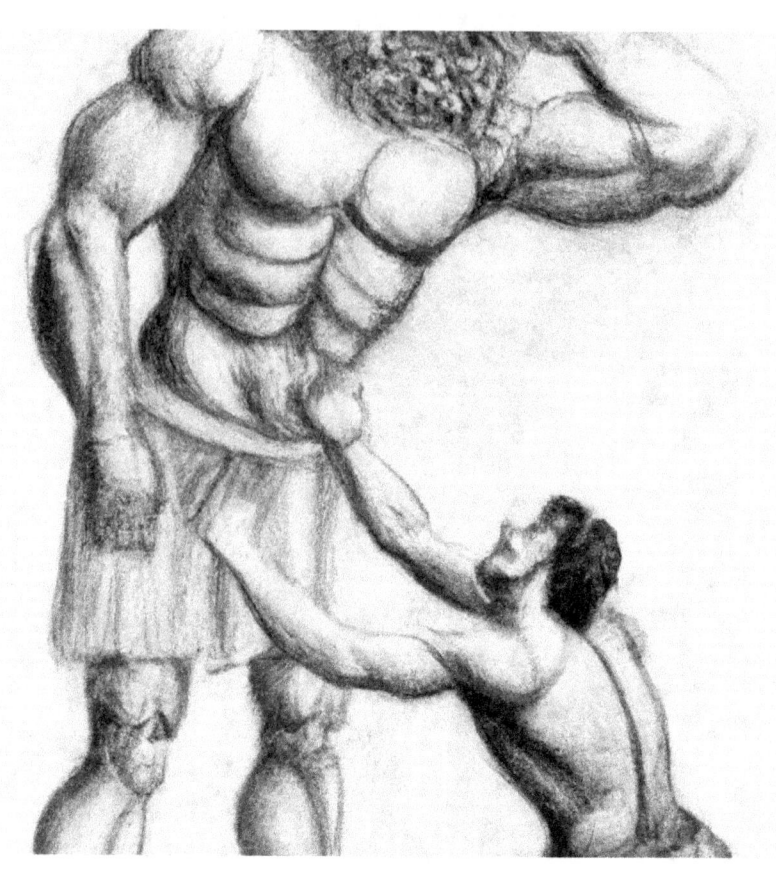

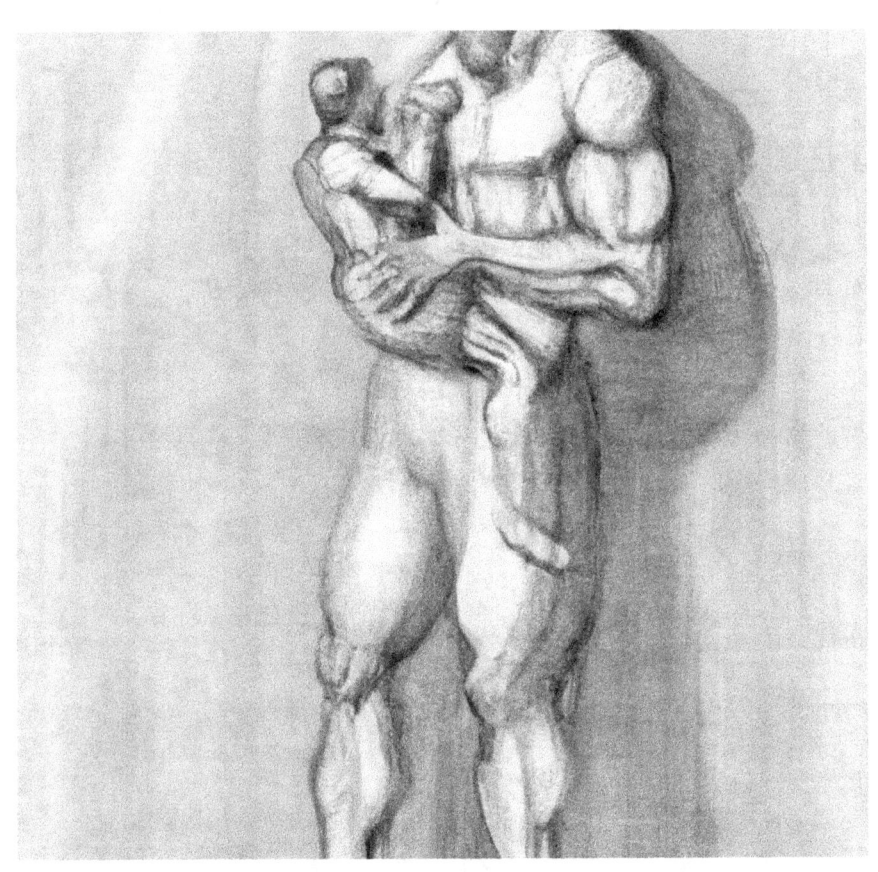

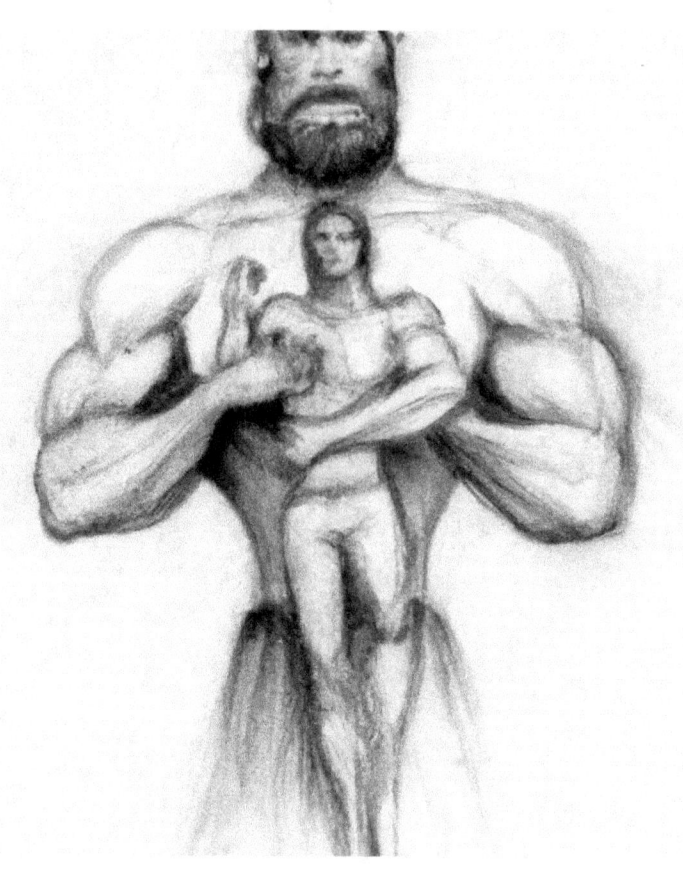

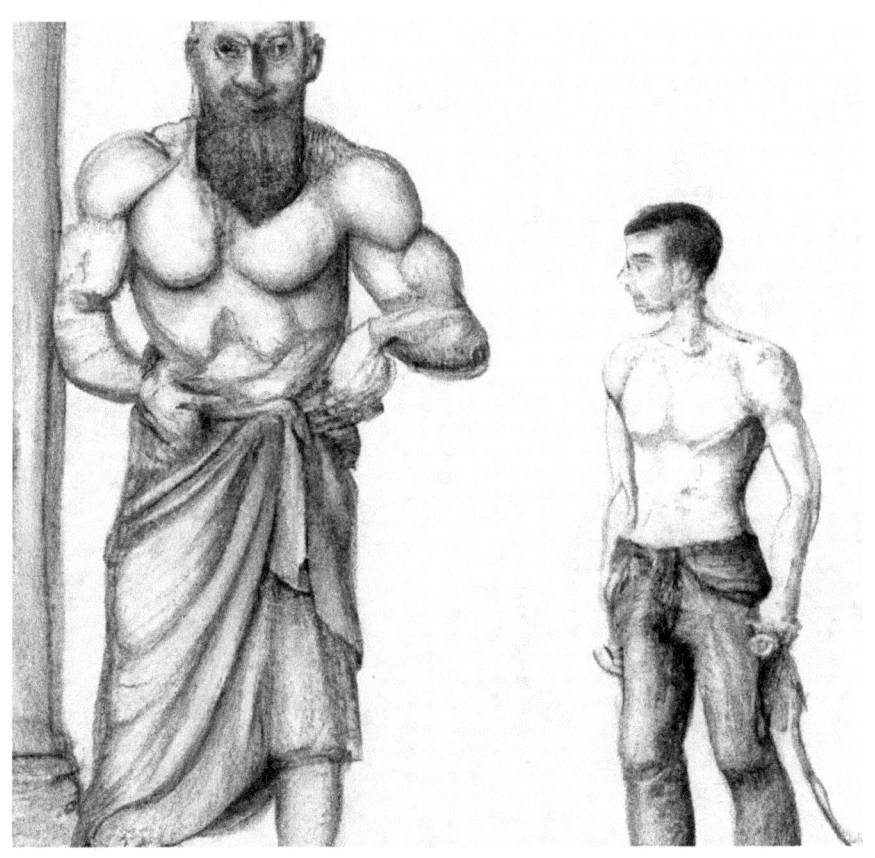

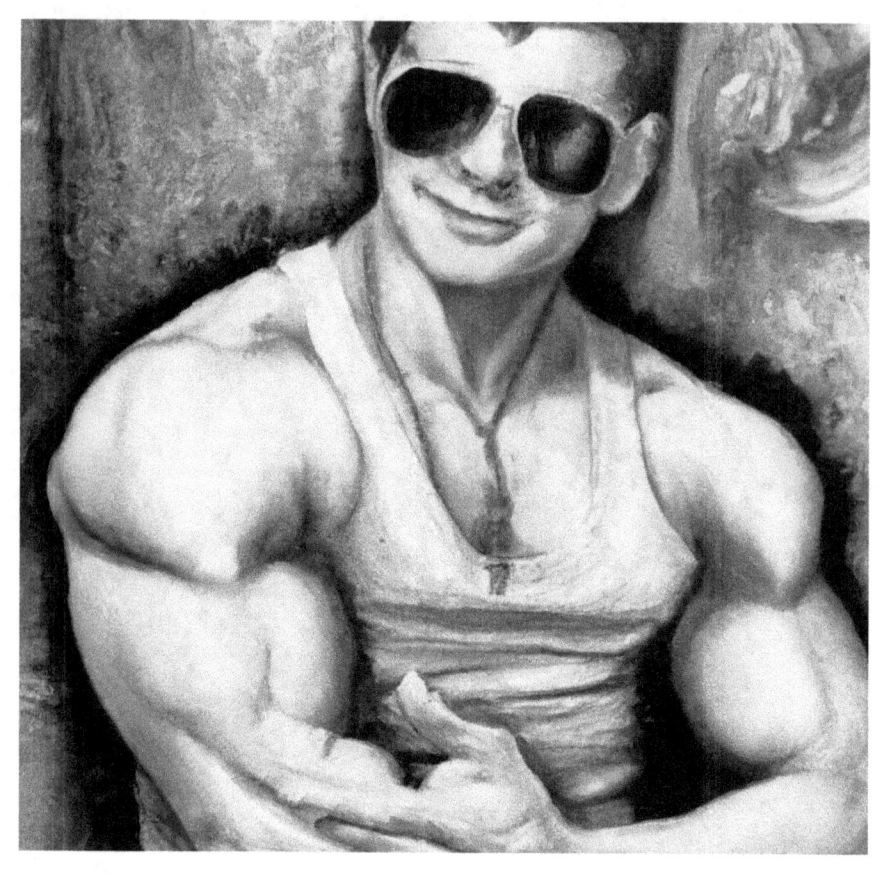

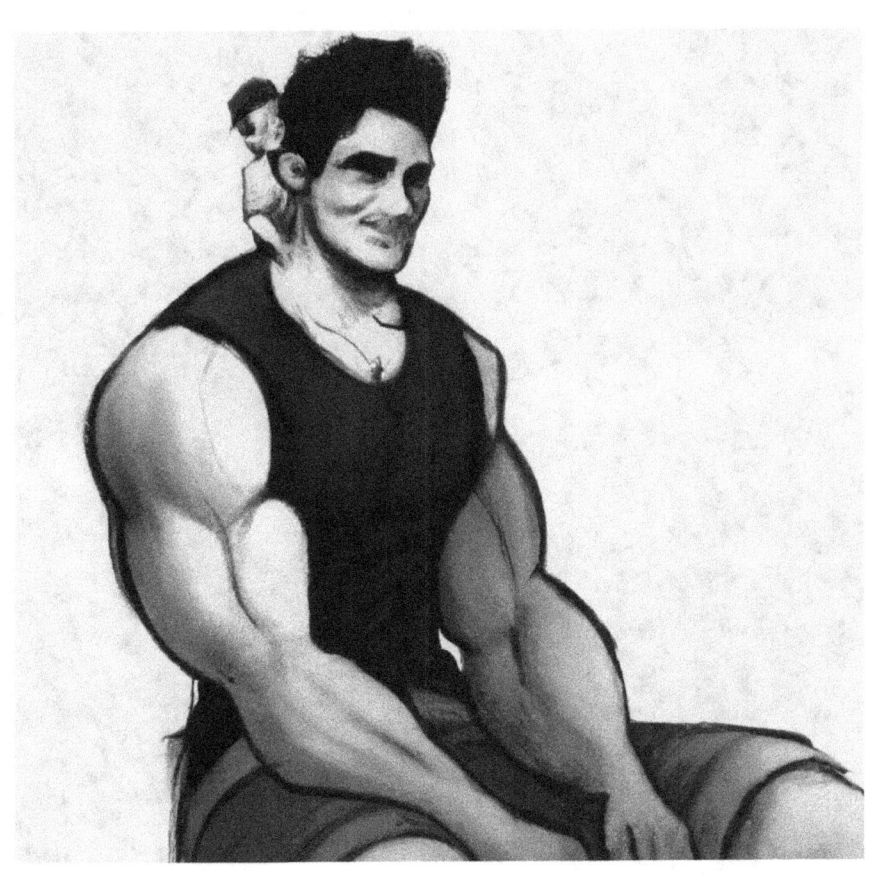

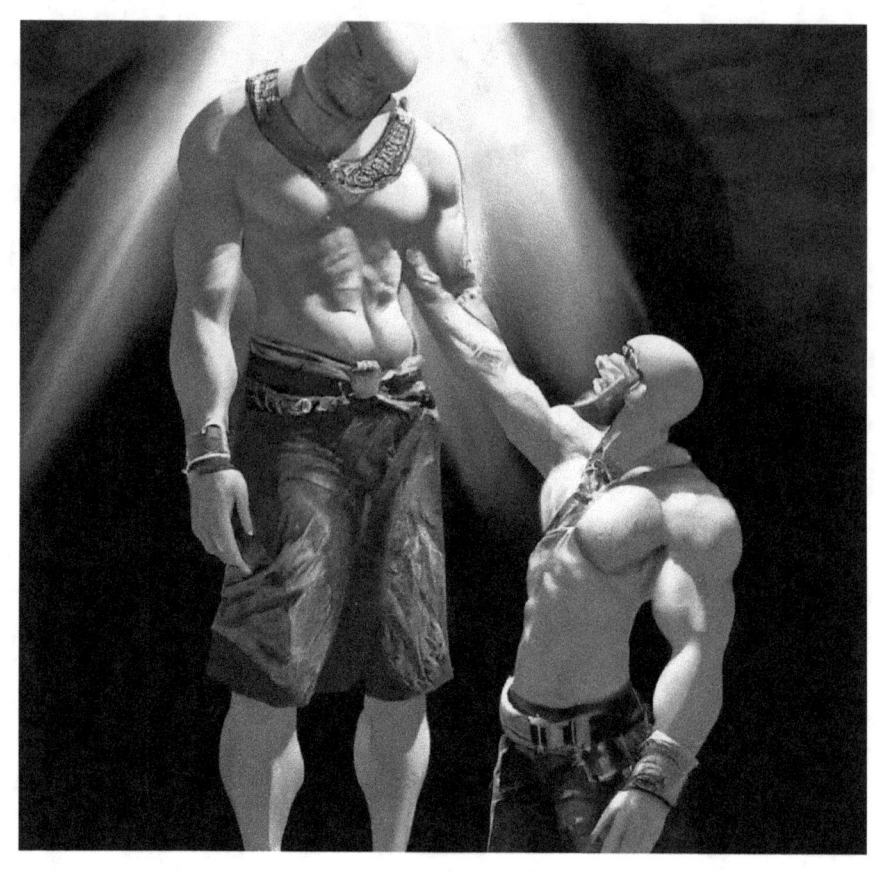

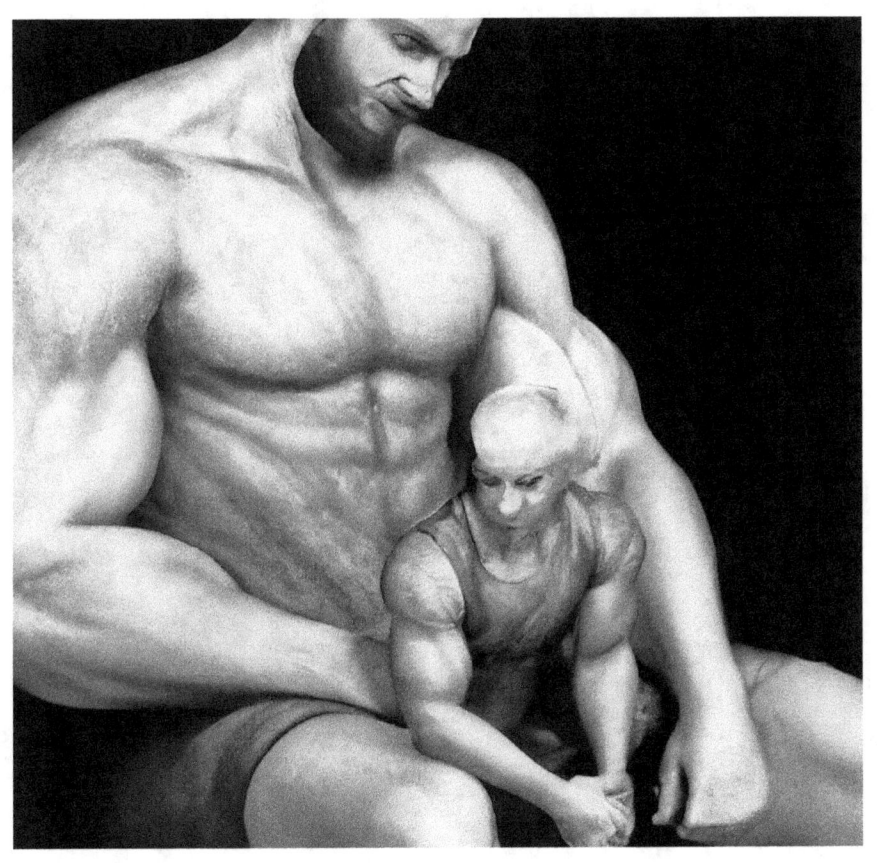

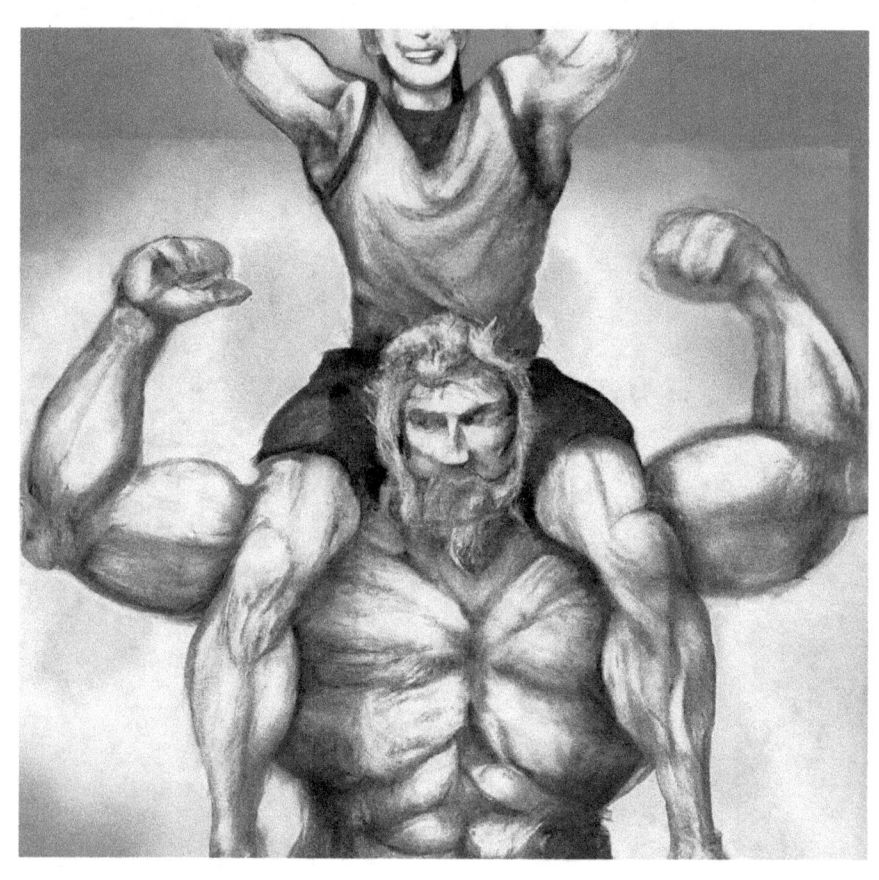

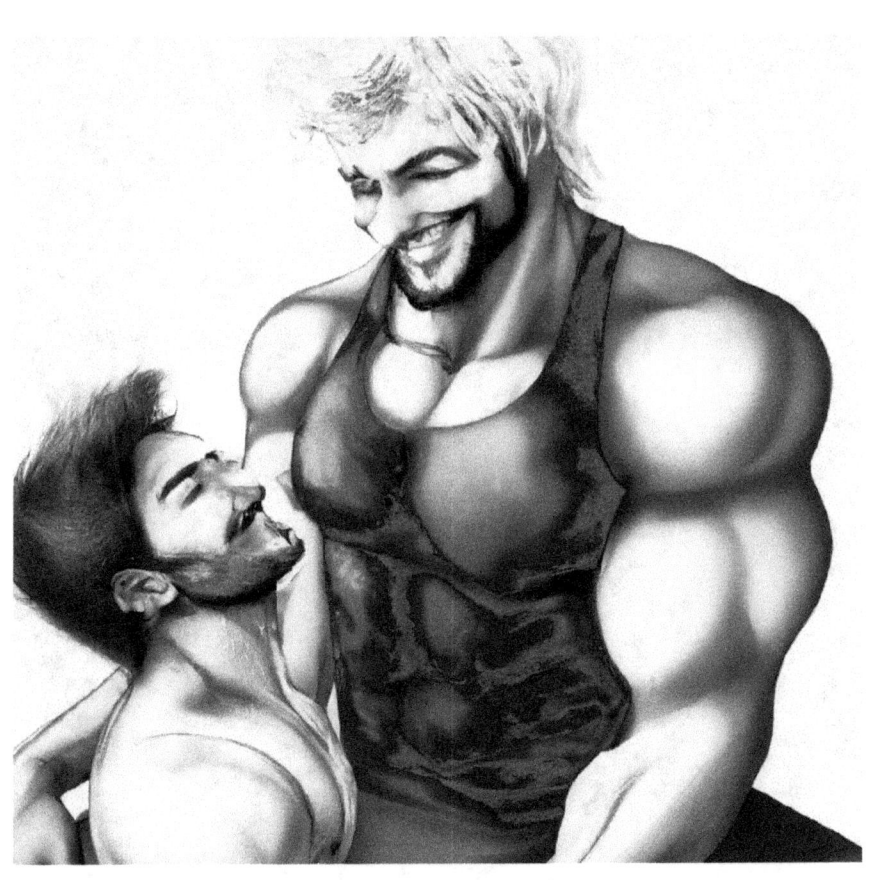

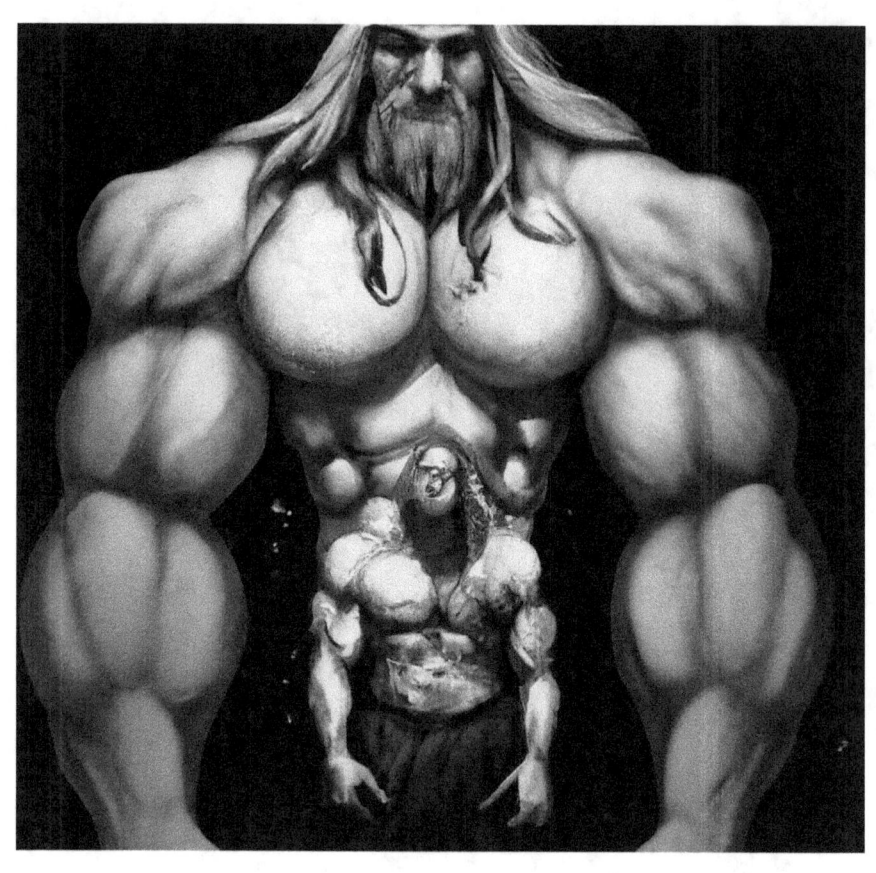

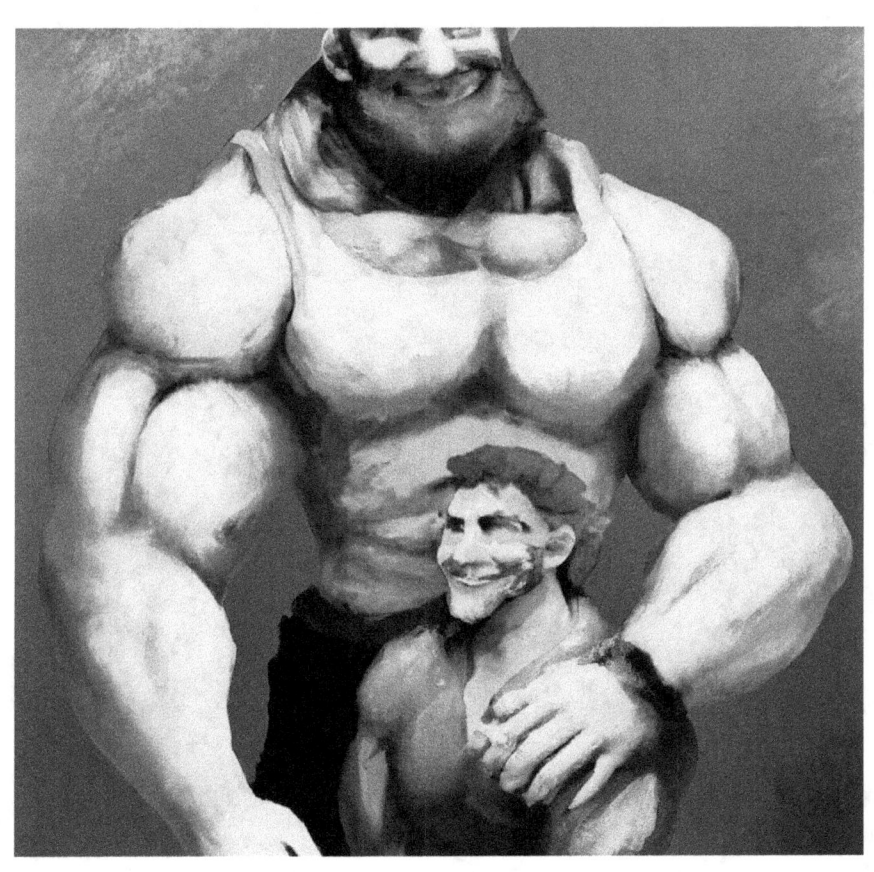

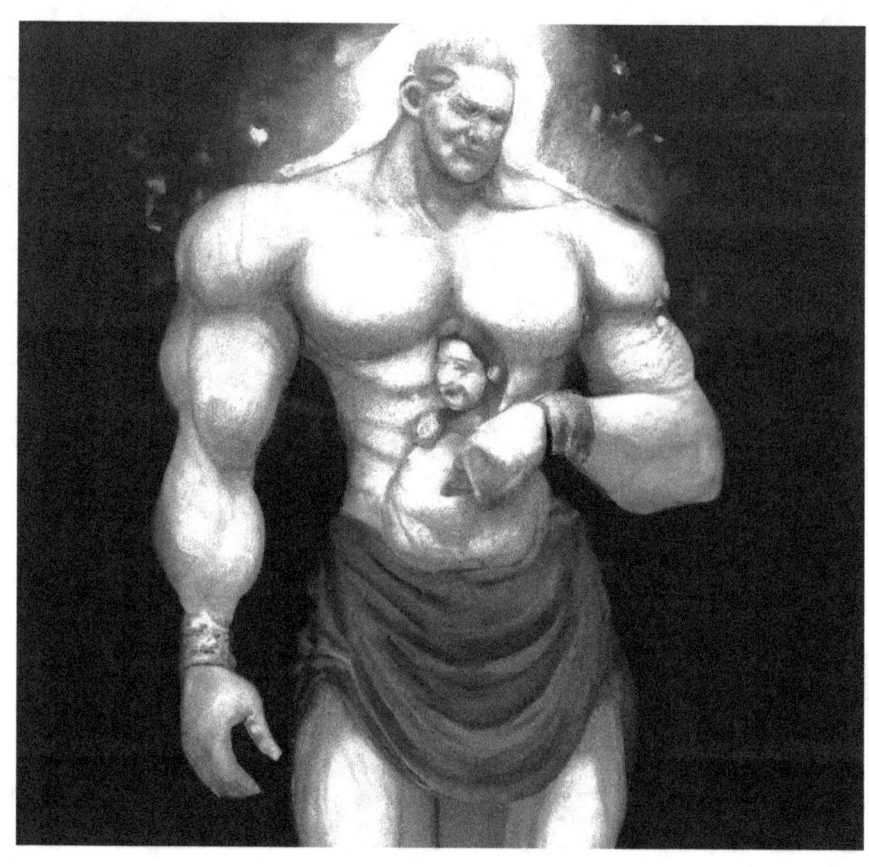

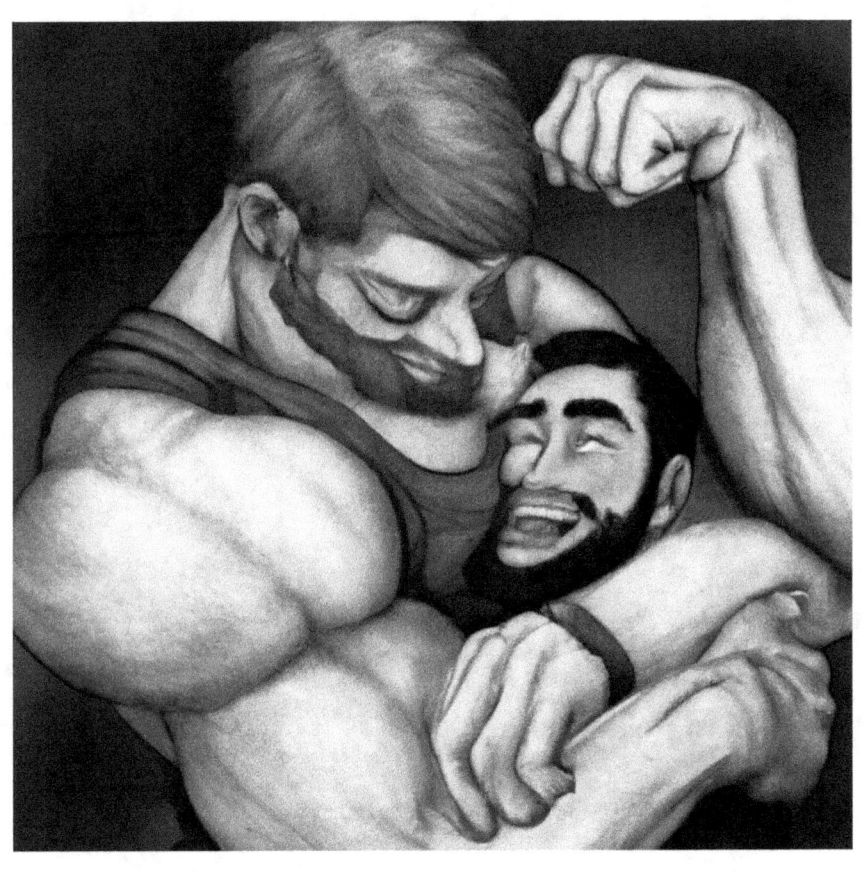

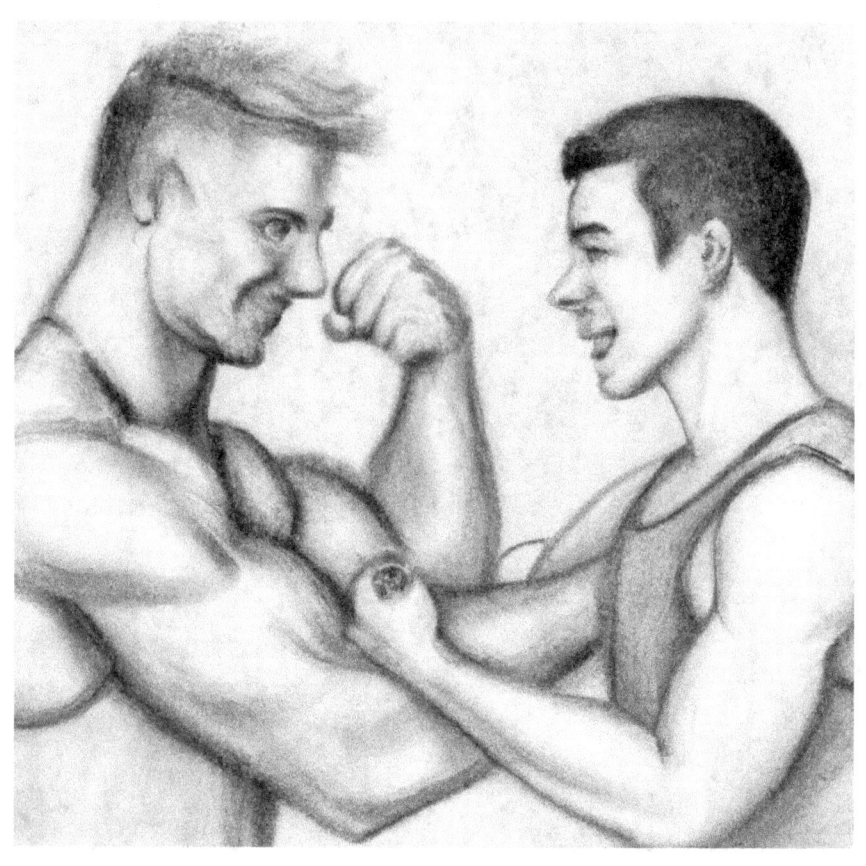

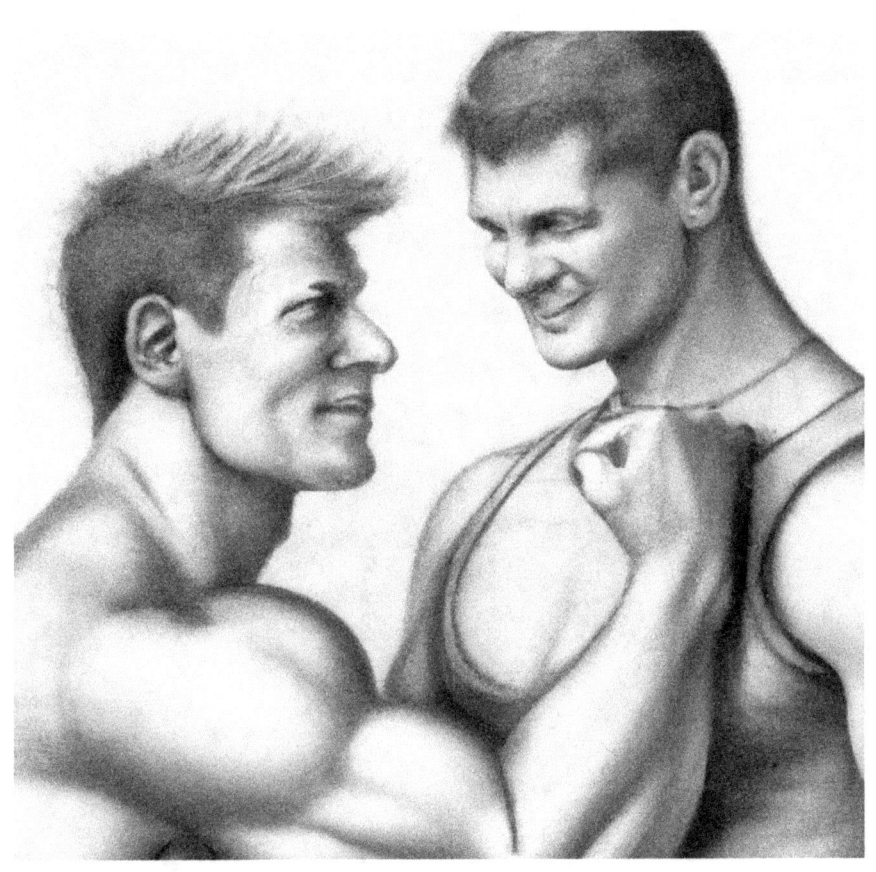

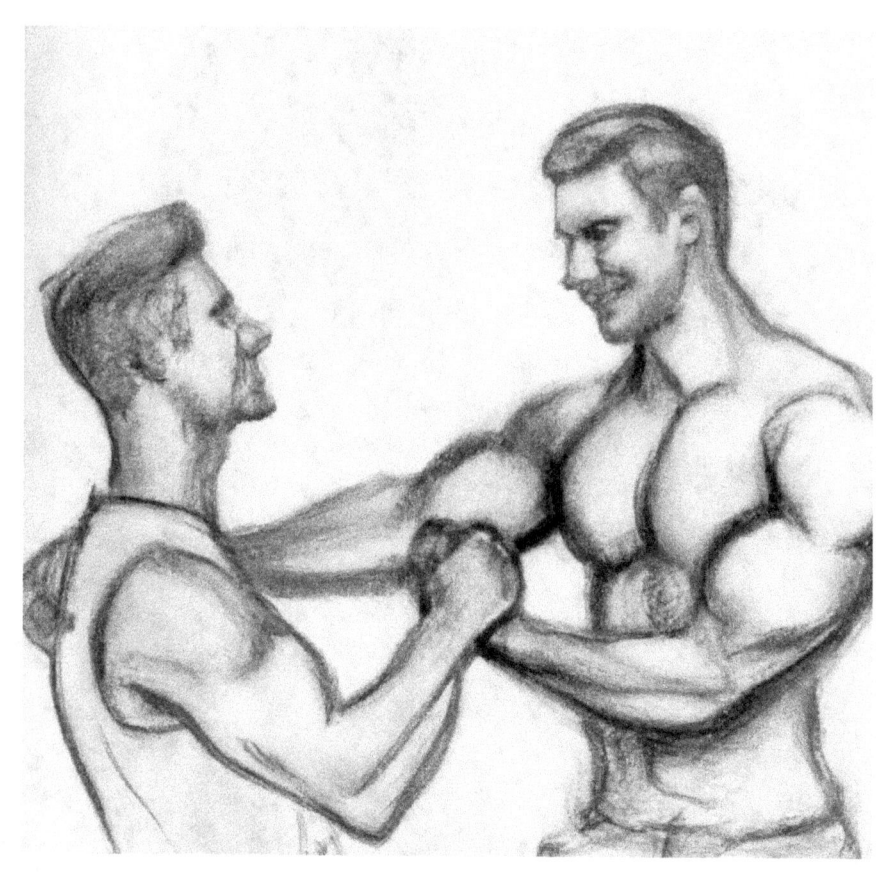

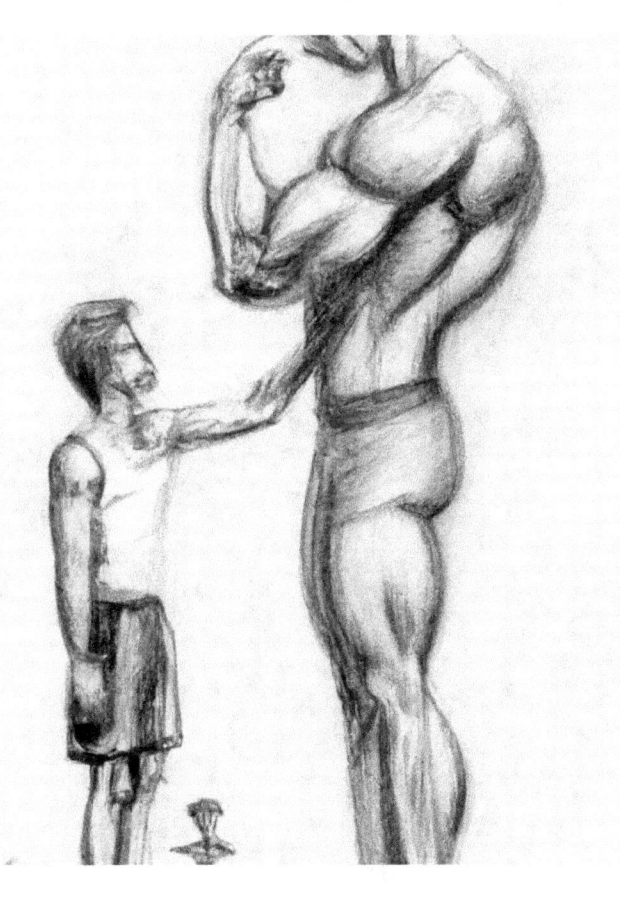

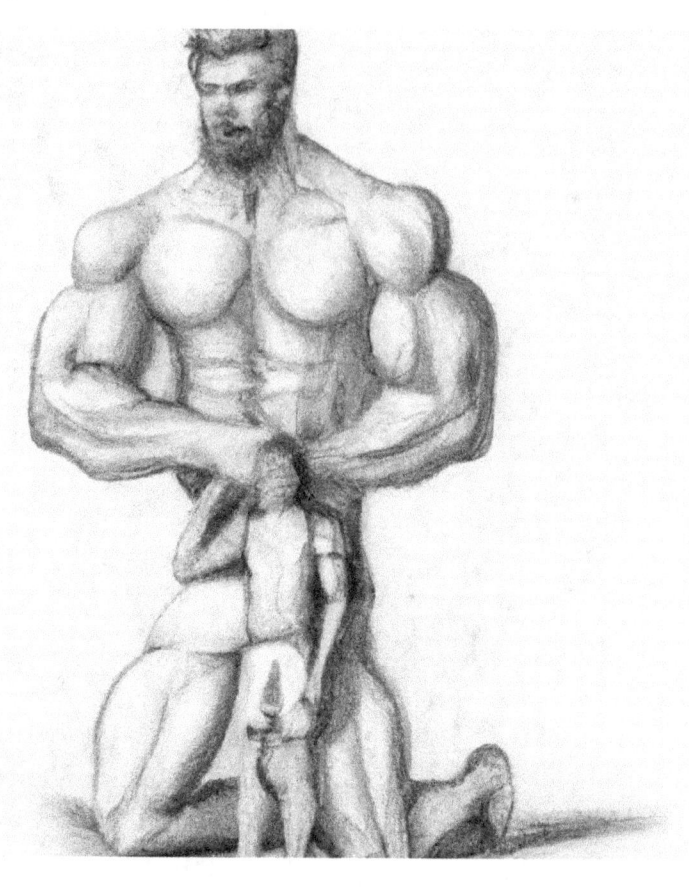

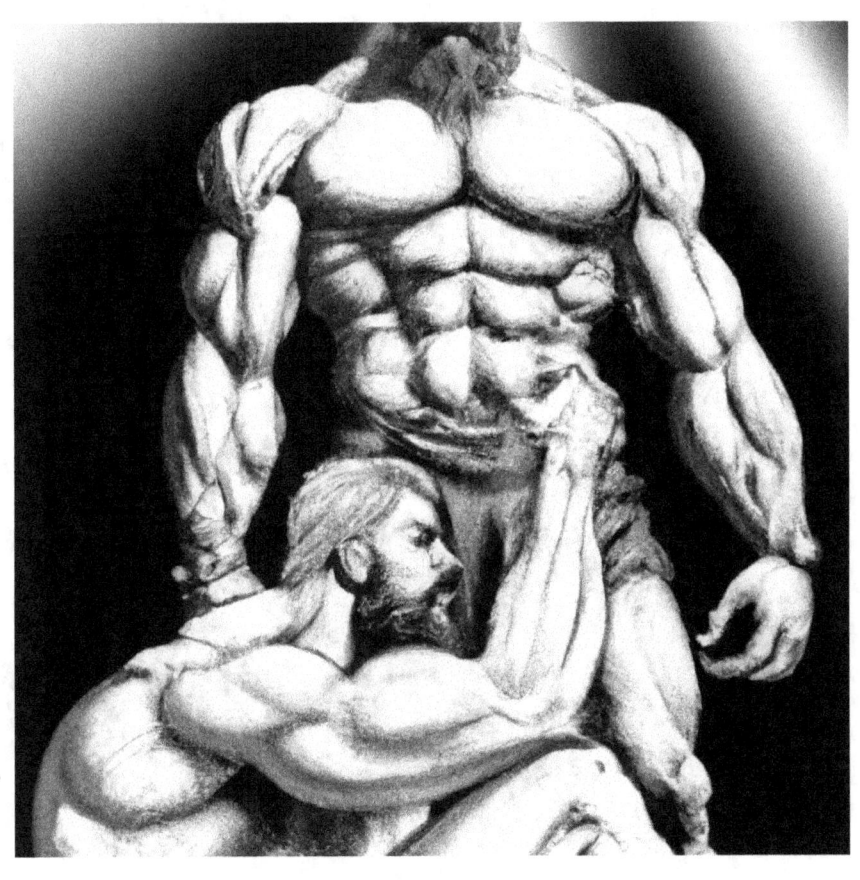

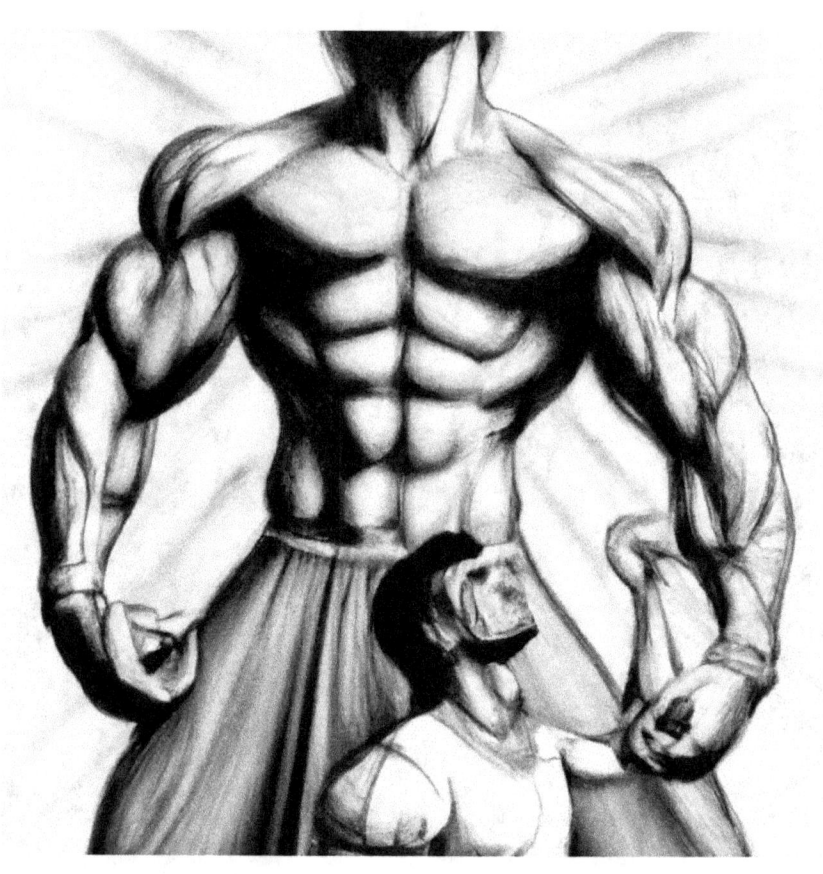

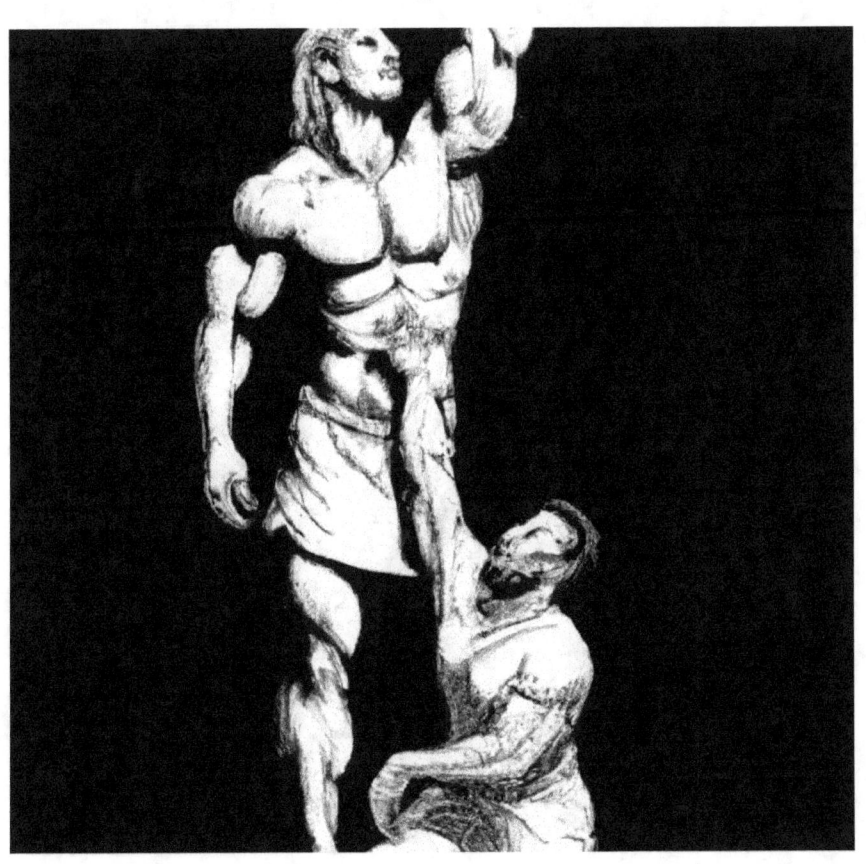

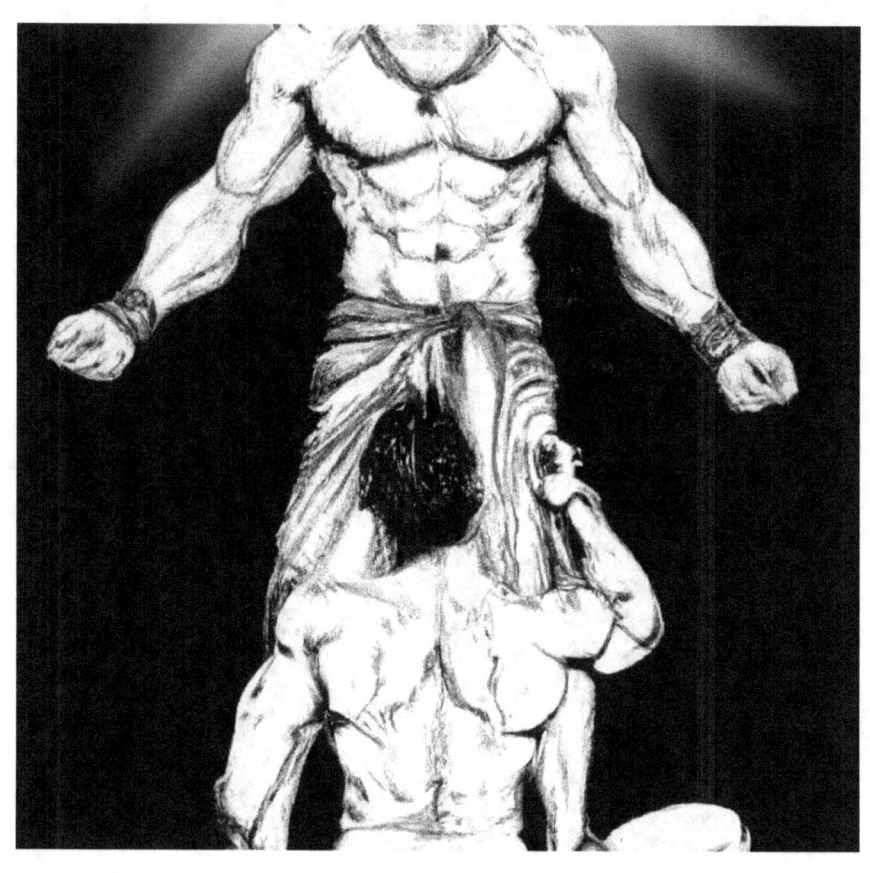

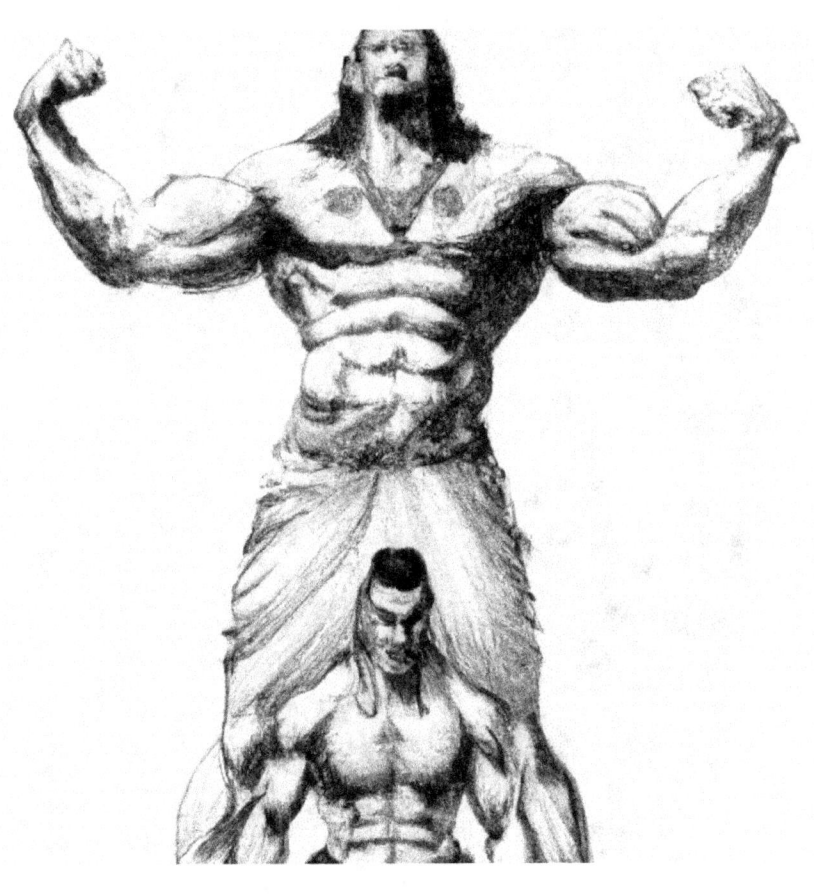

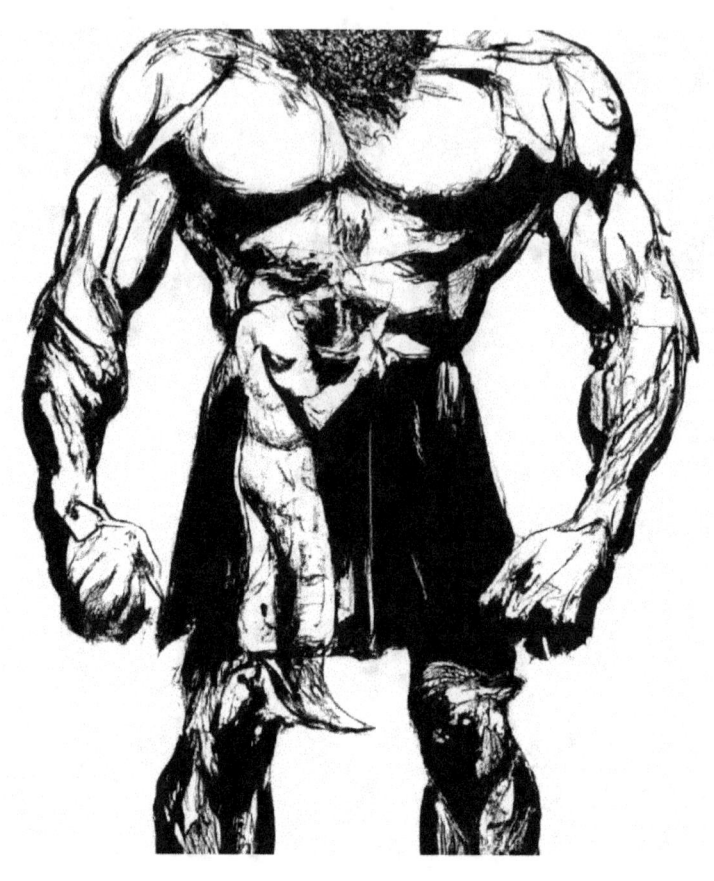

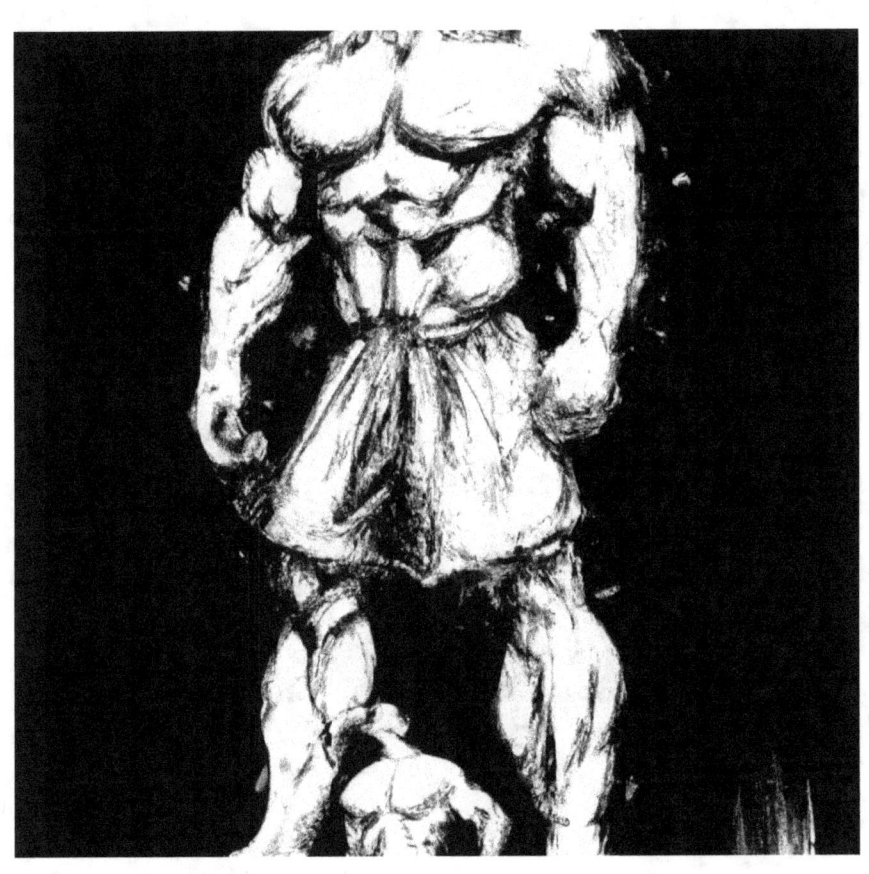

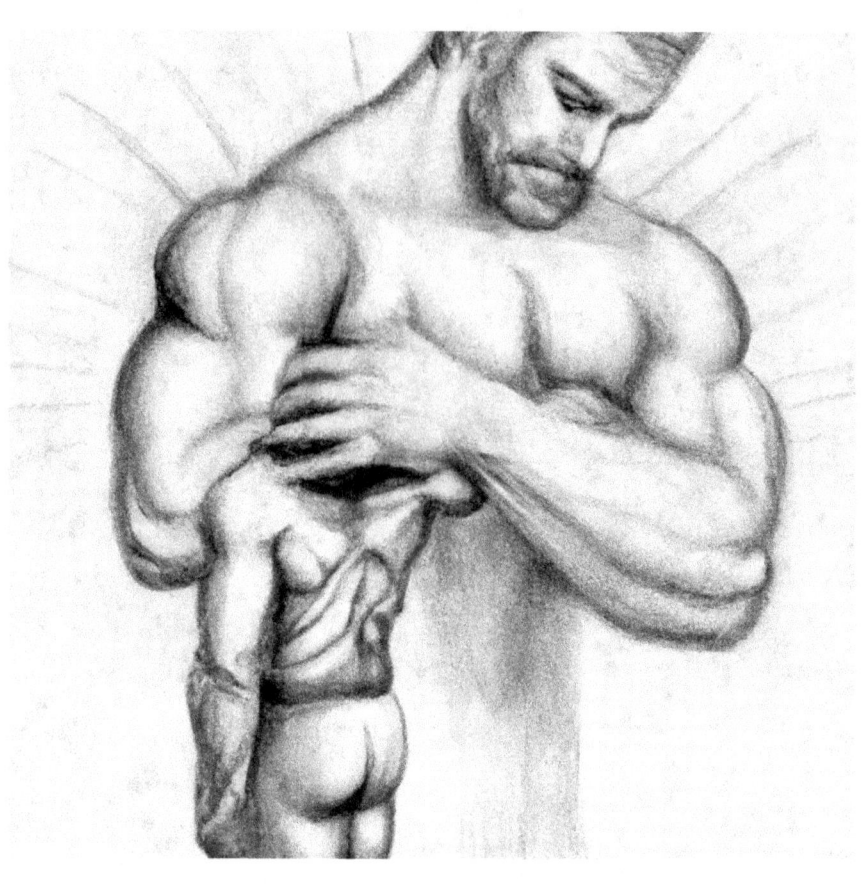

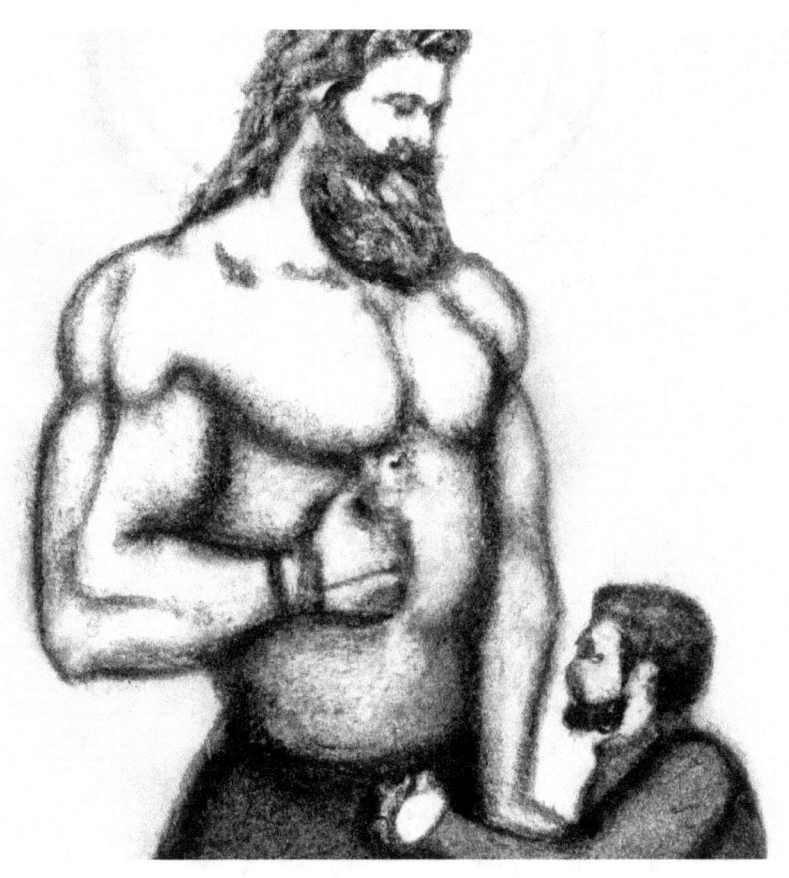

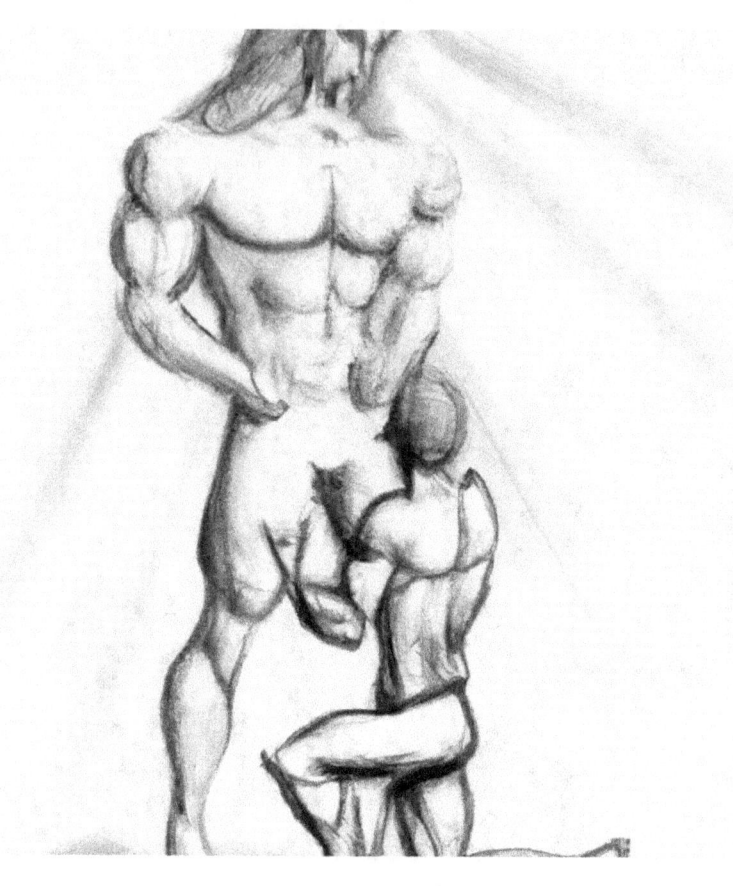

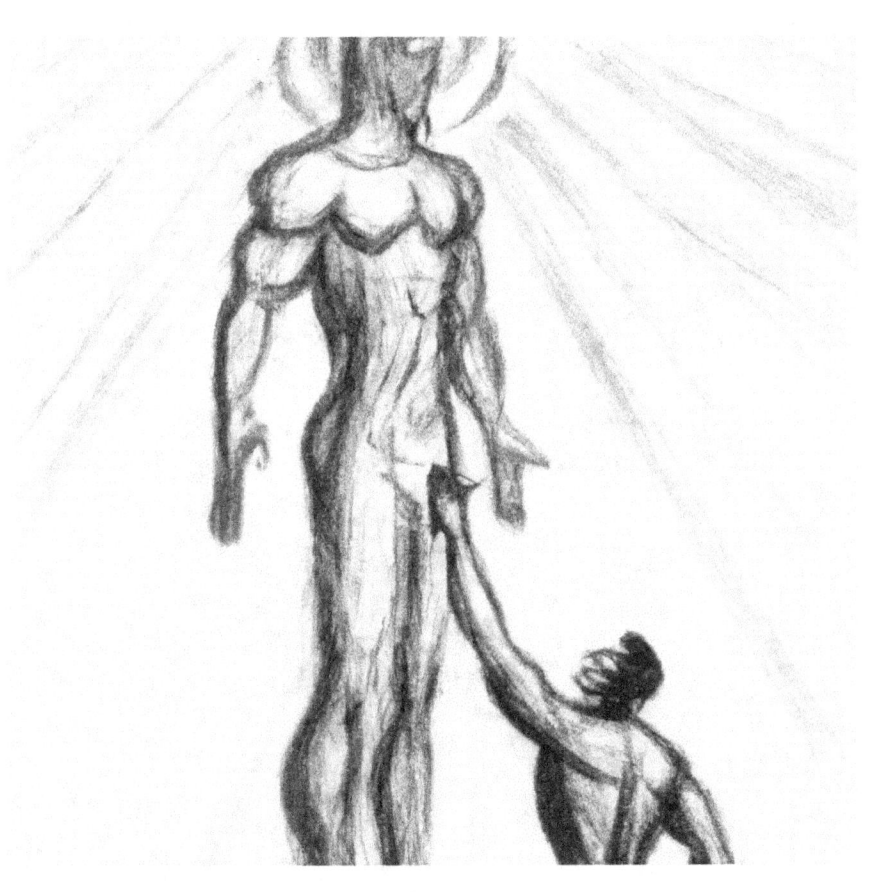

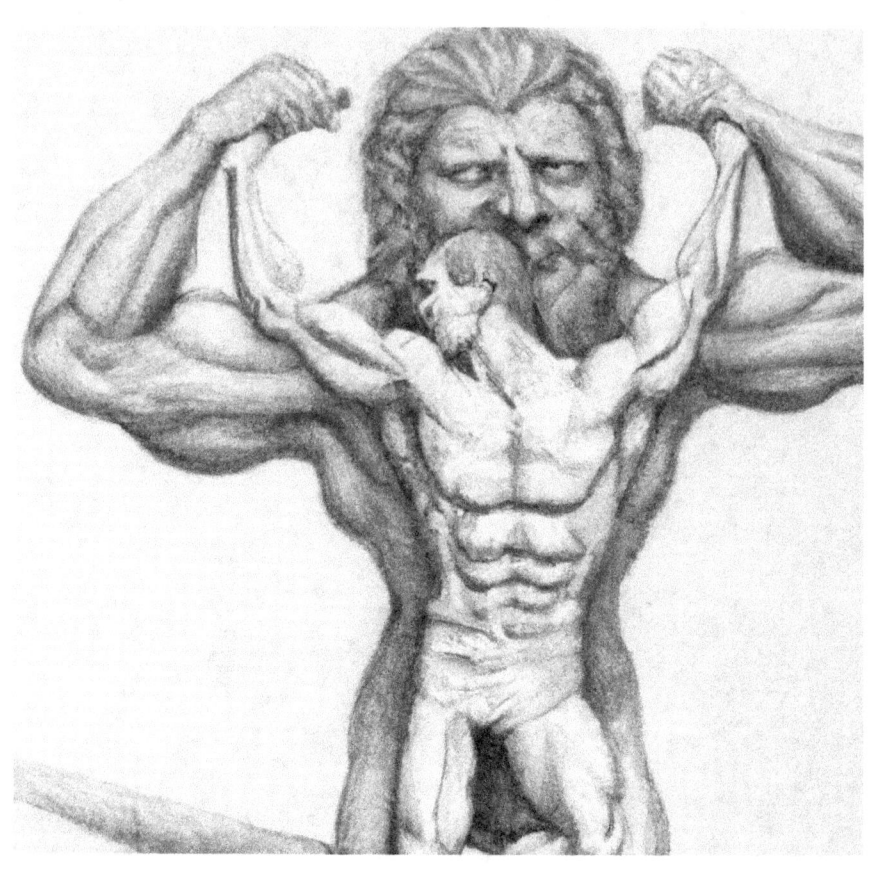

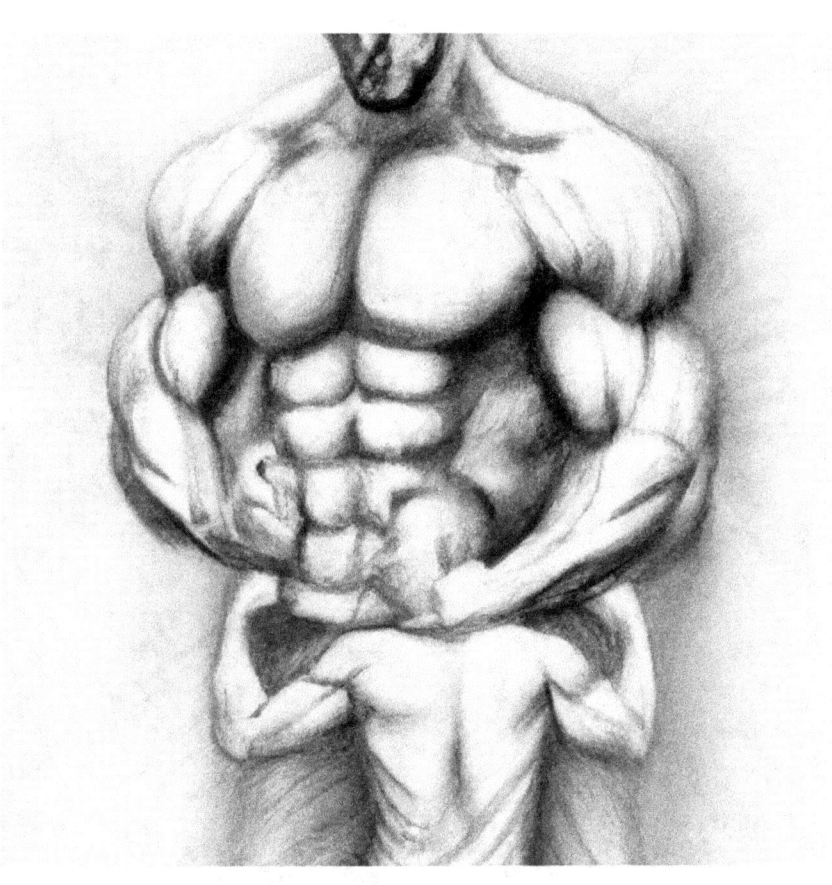

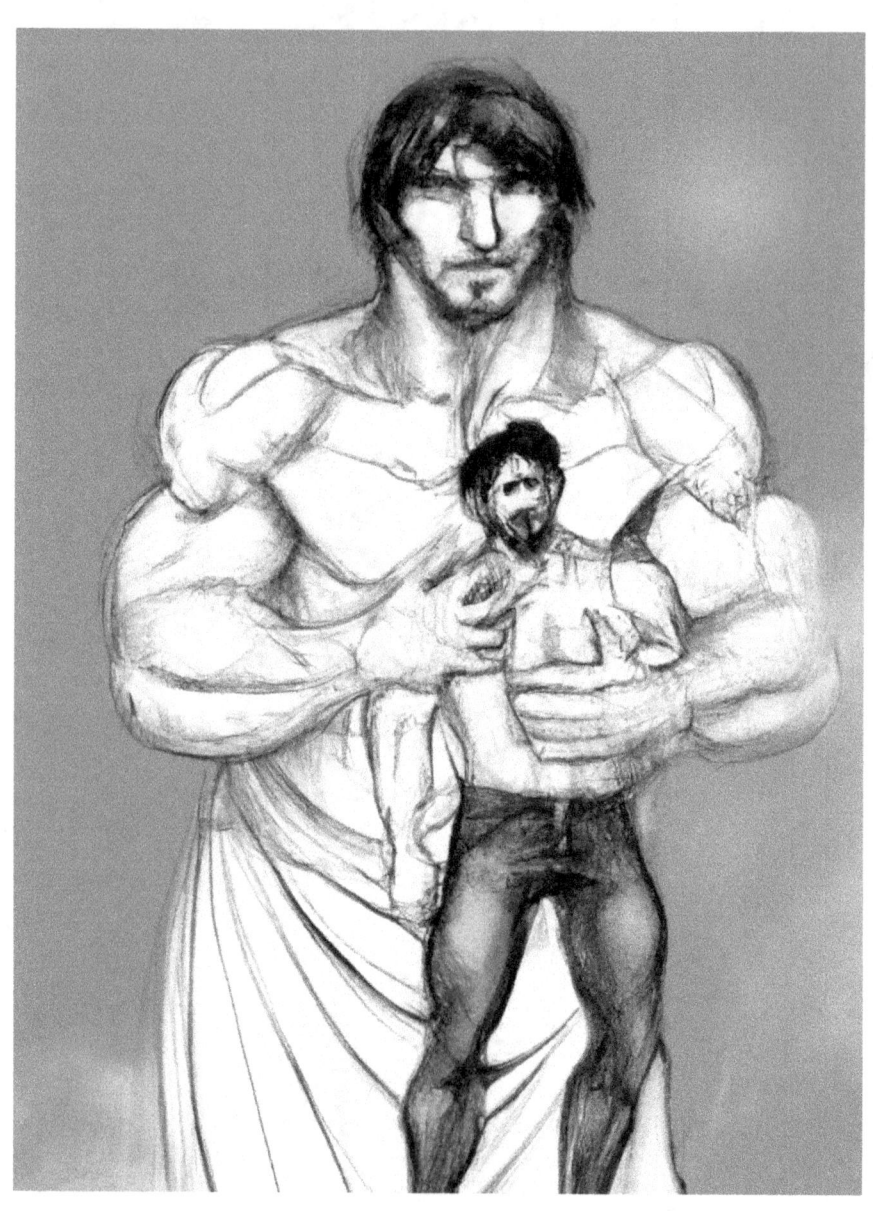

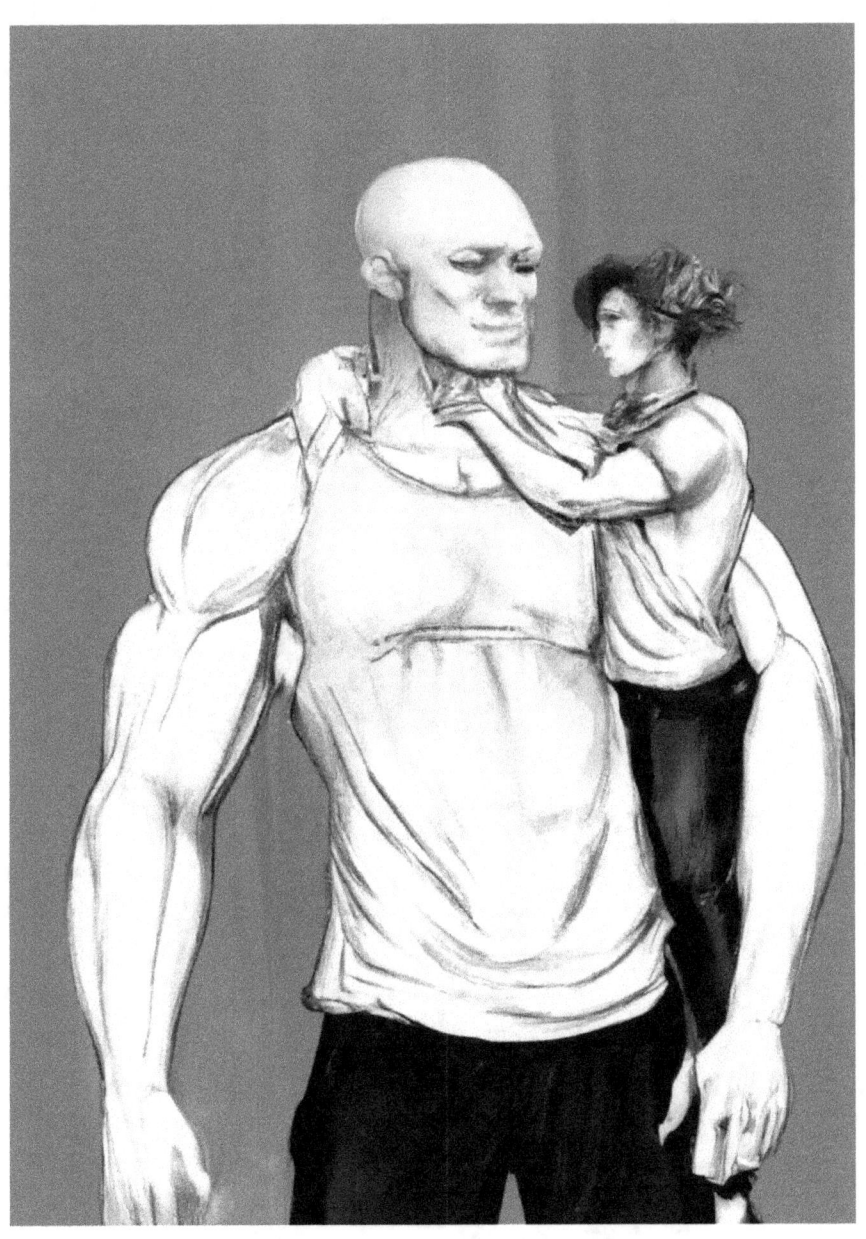

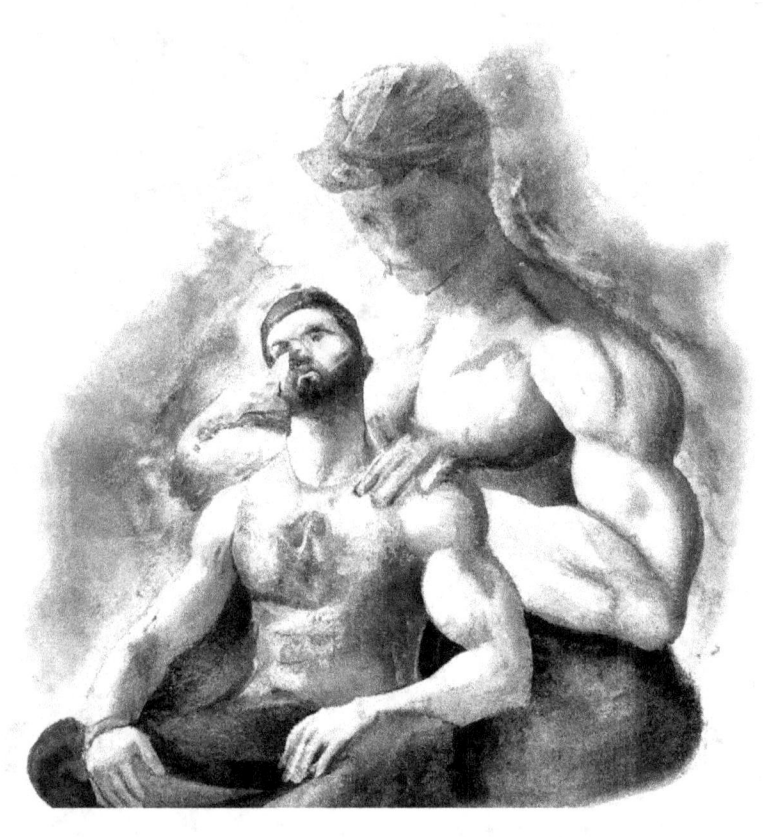

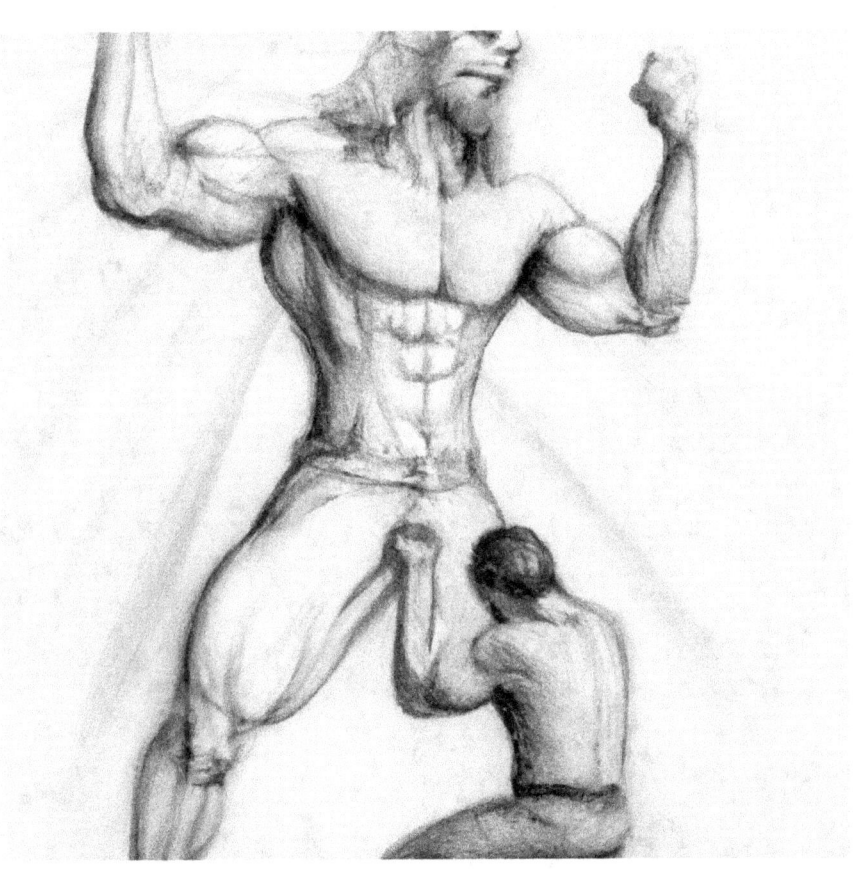

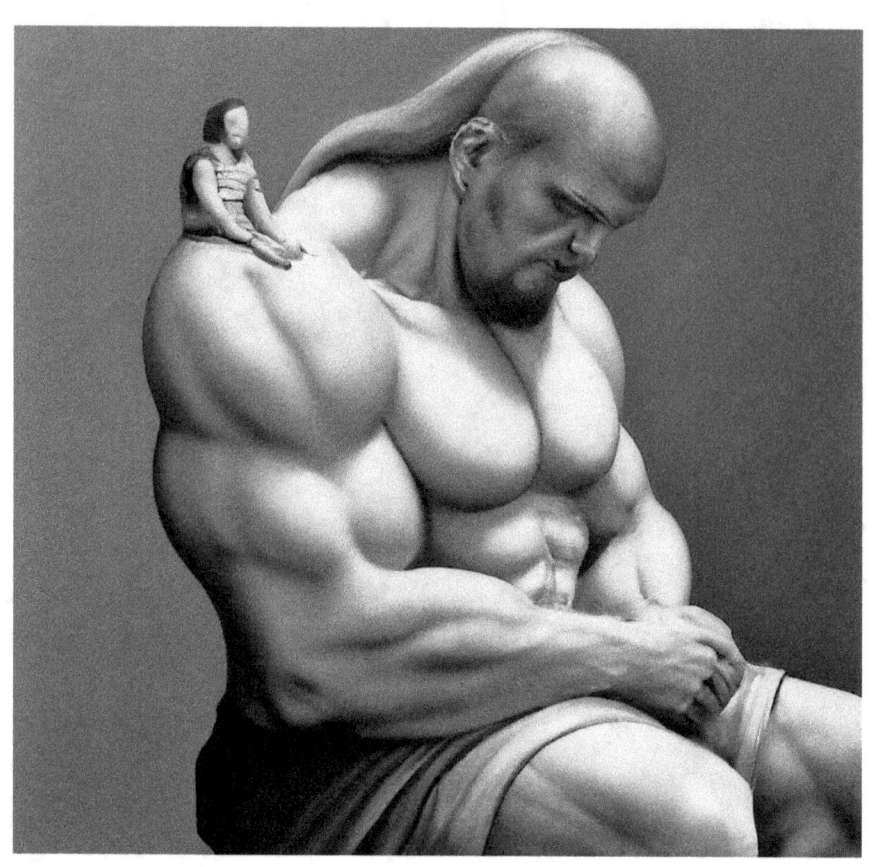

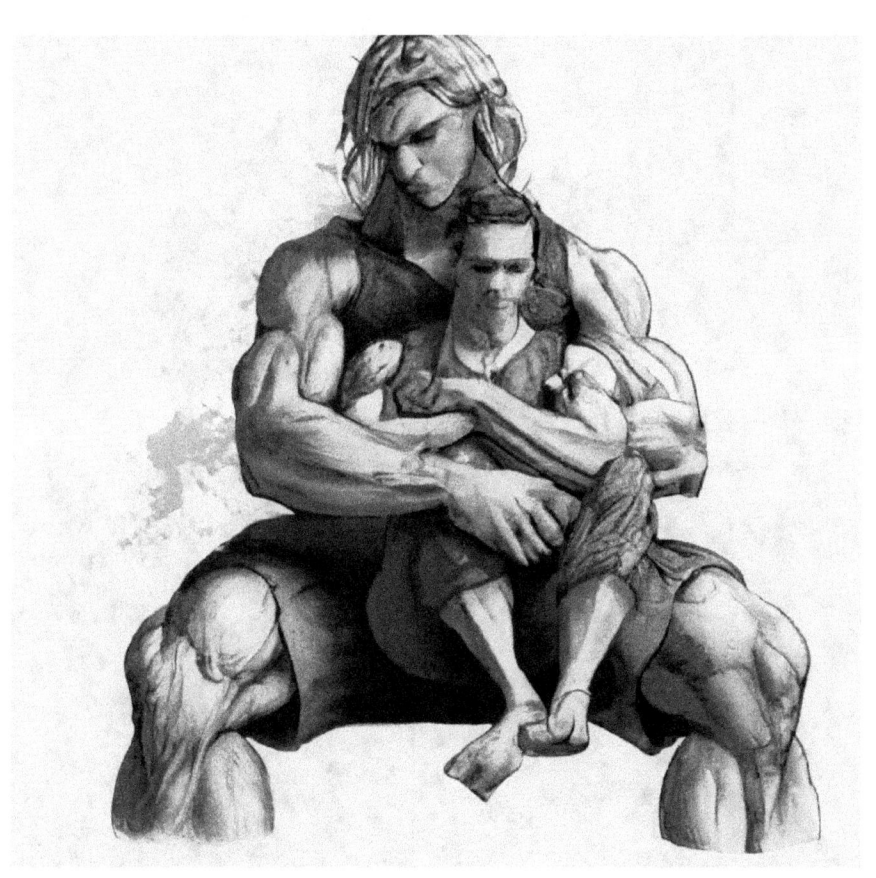

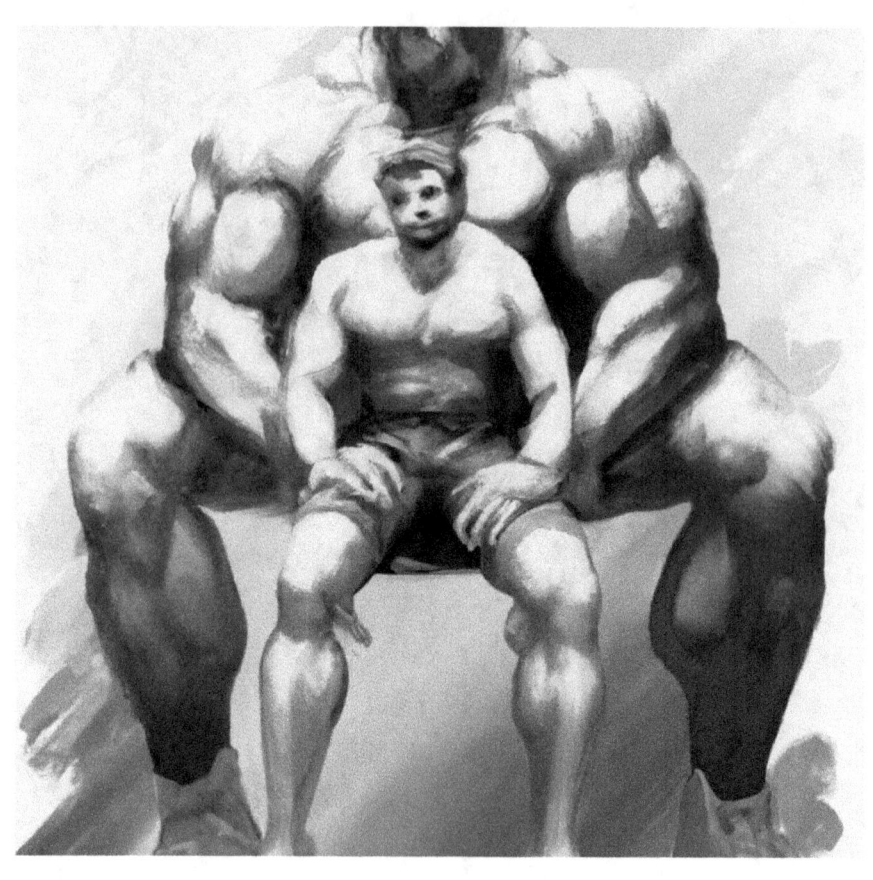

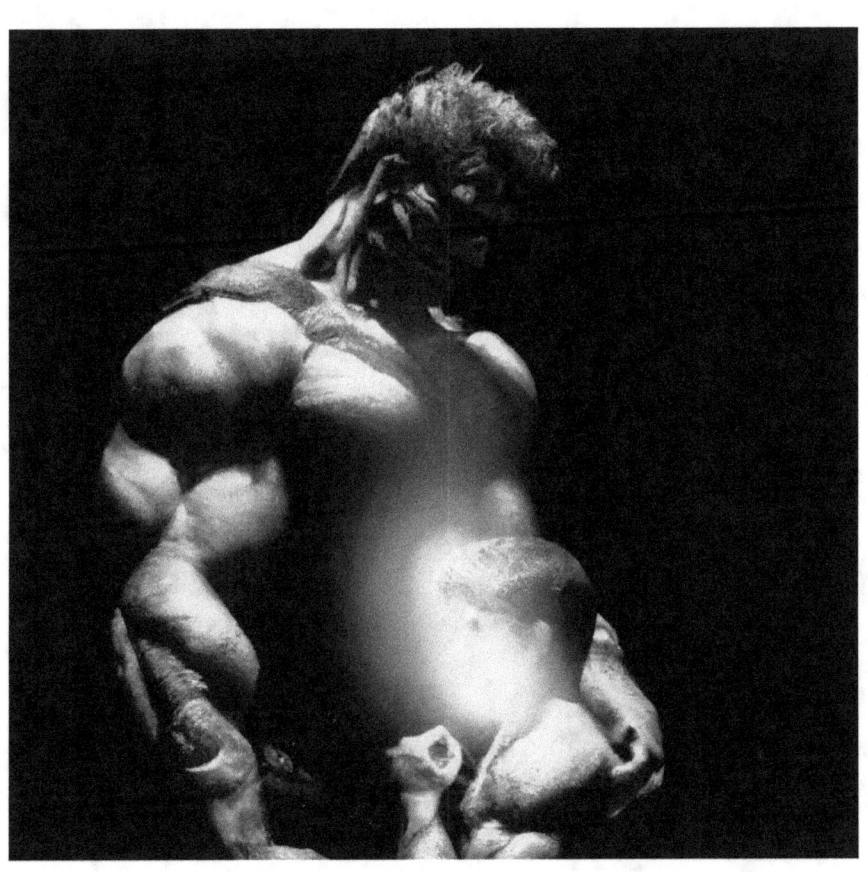

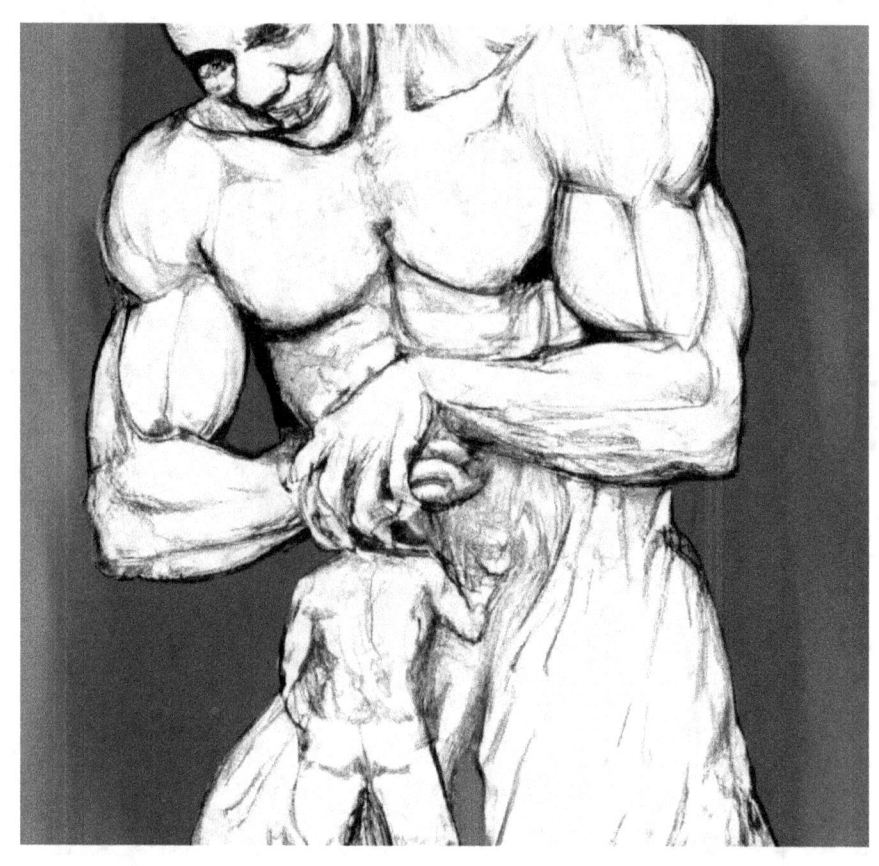

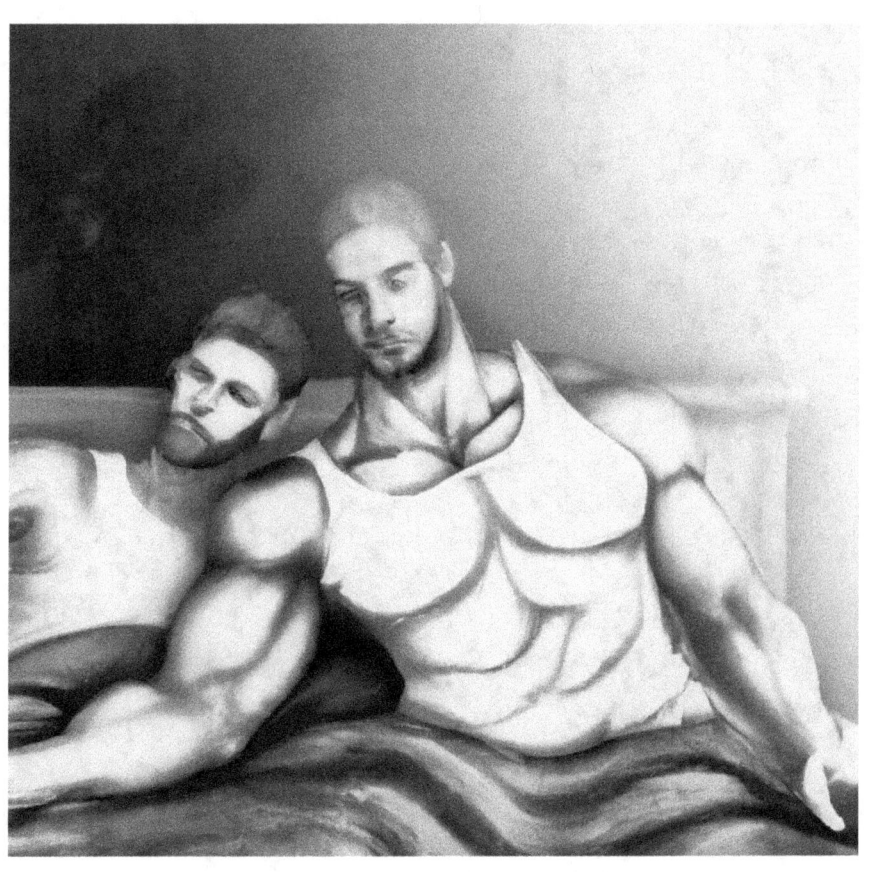

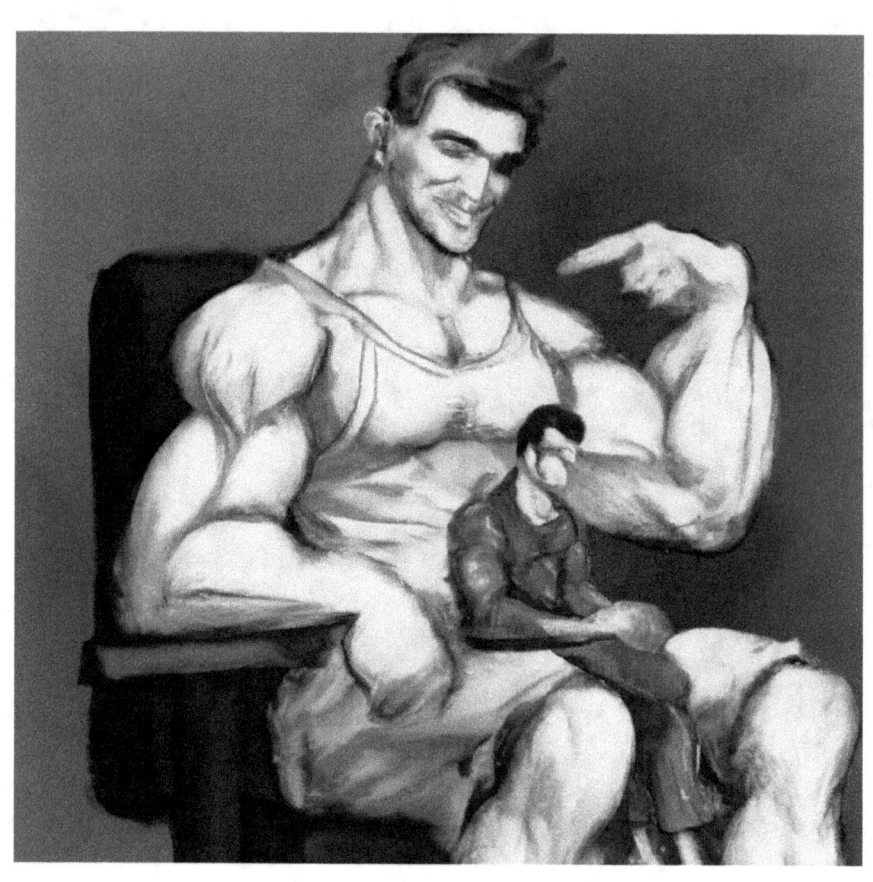

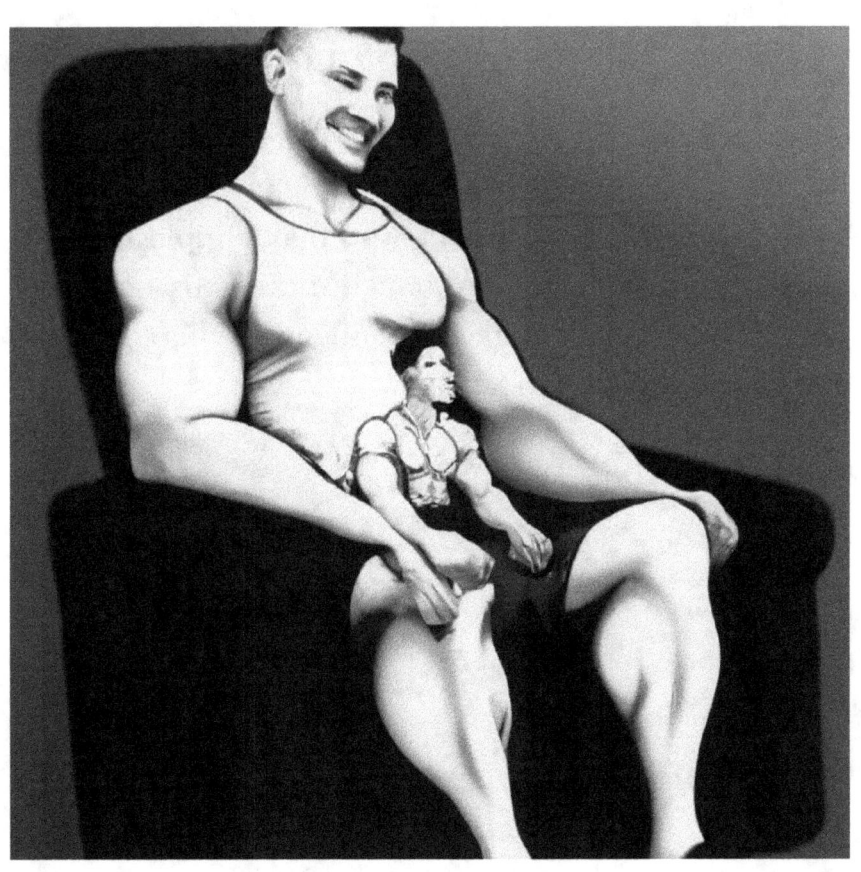

Gods of Stone

This portion of the book is deticated to the ancient muscular gods that once lived amoung us. They were worshipped by our ancesters, who built temples to them and learned their ways. Although these gods no longer walk the earth, their stone momuments are here for us to admire and worship today.

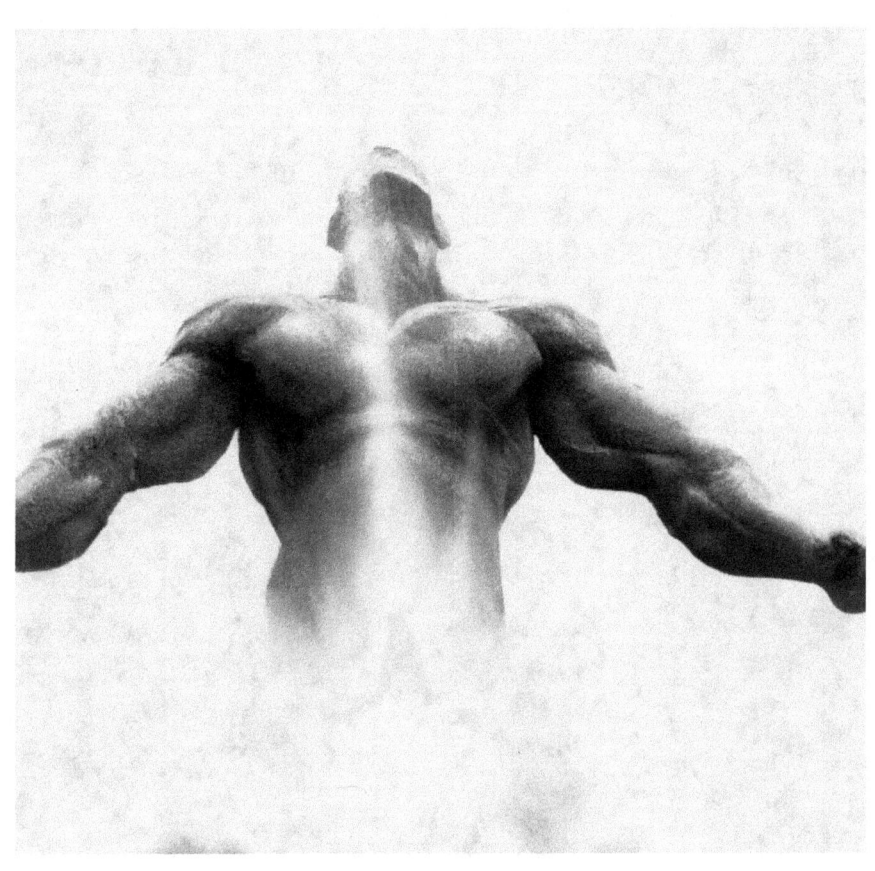

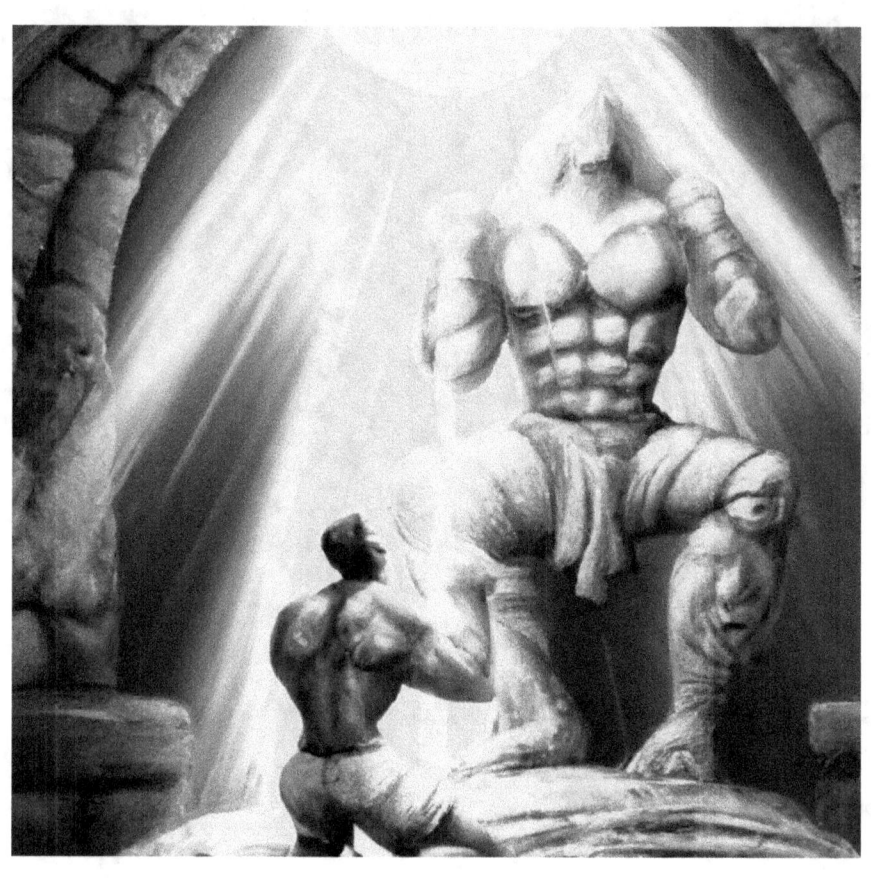

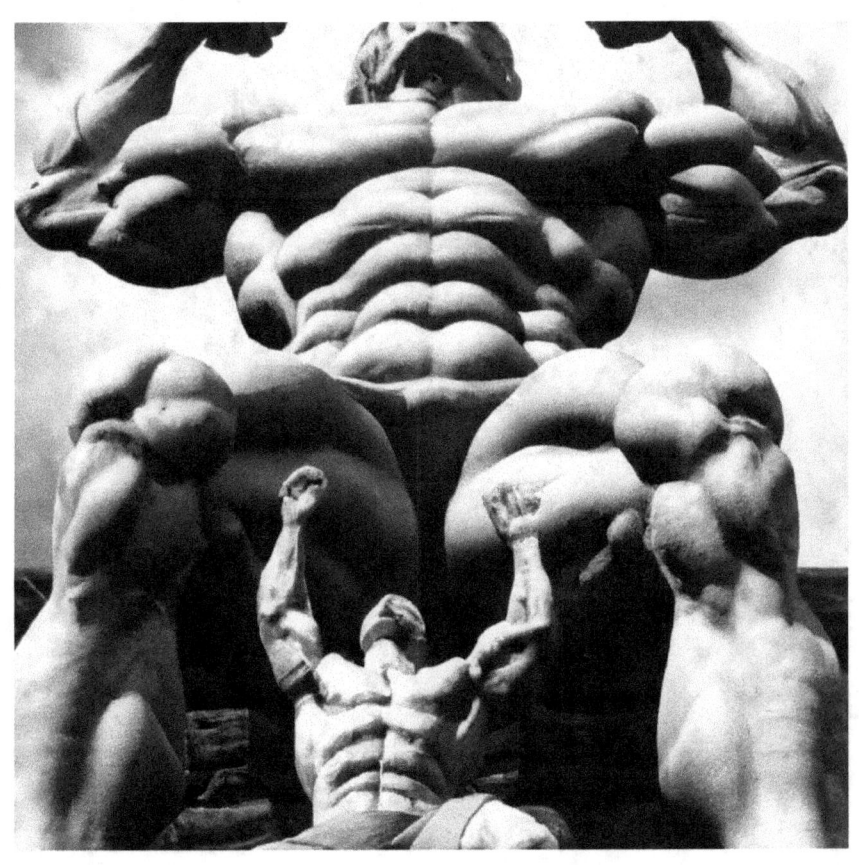

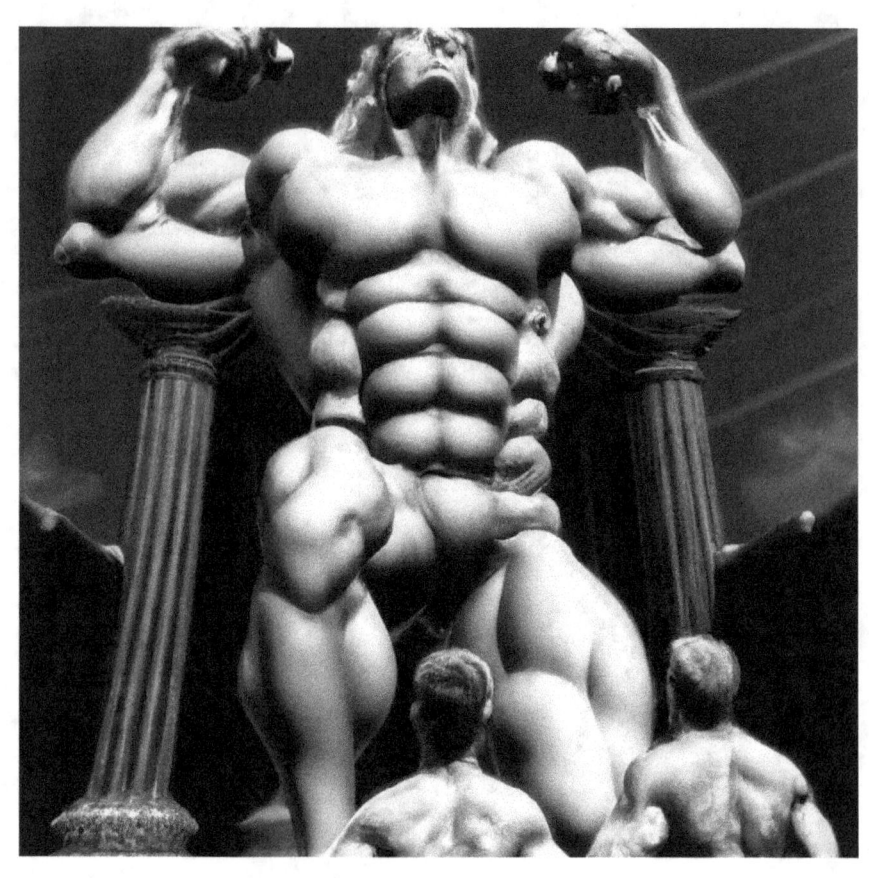

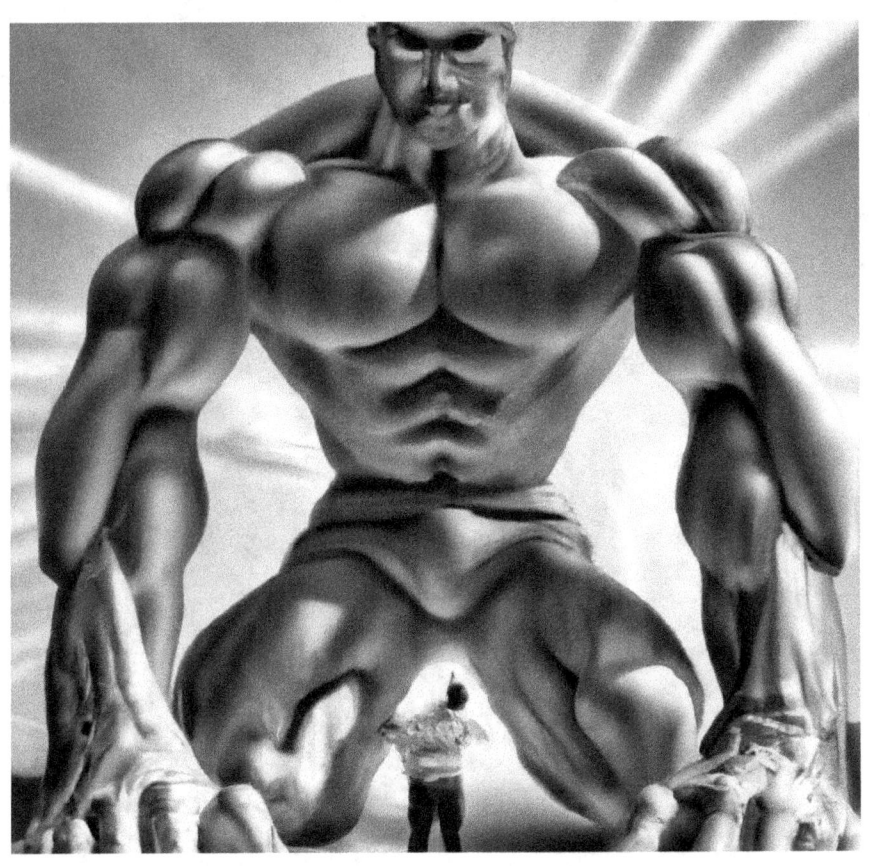

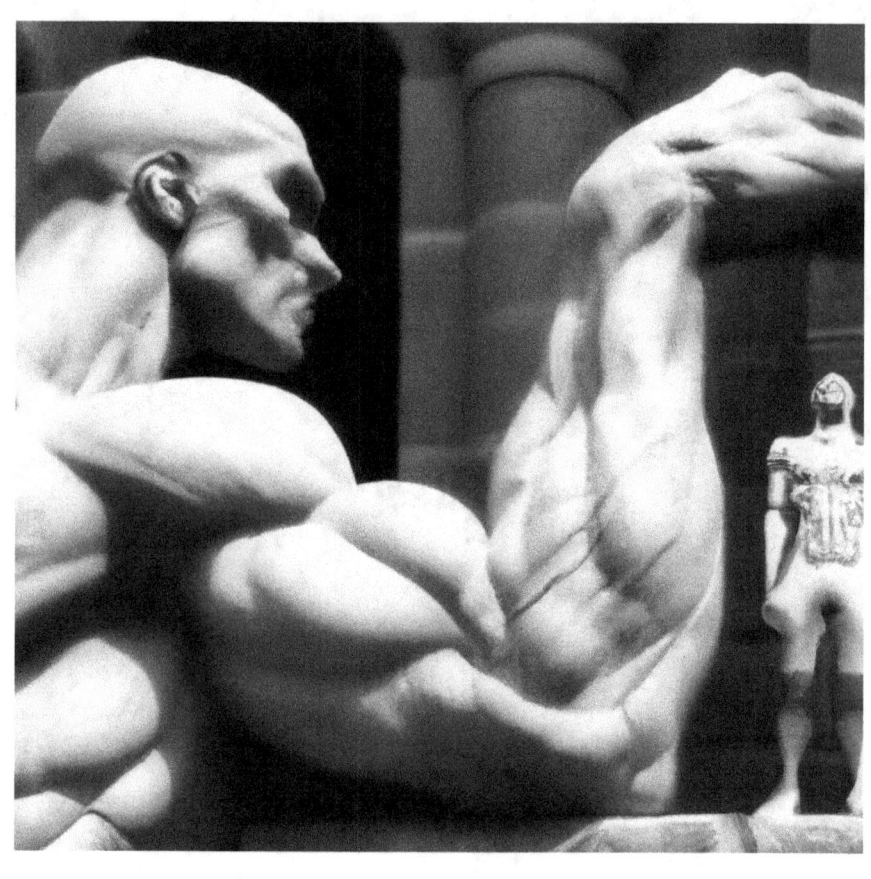

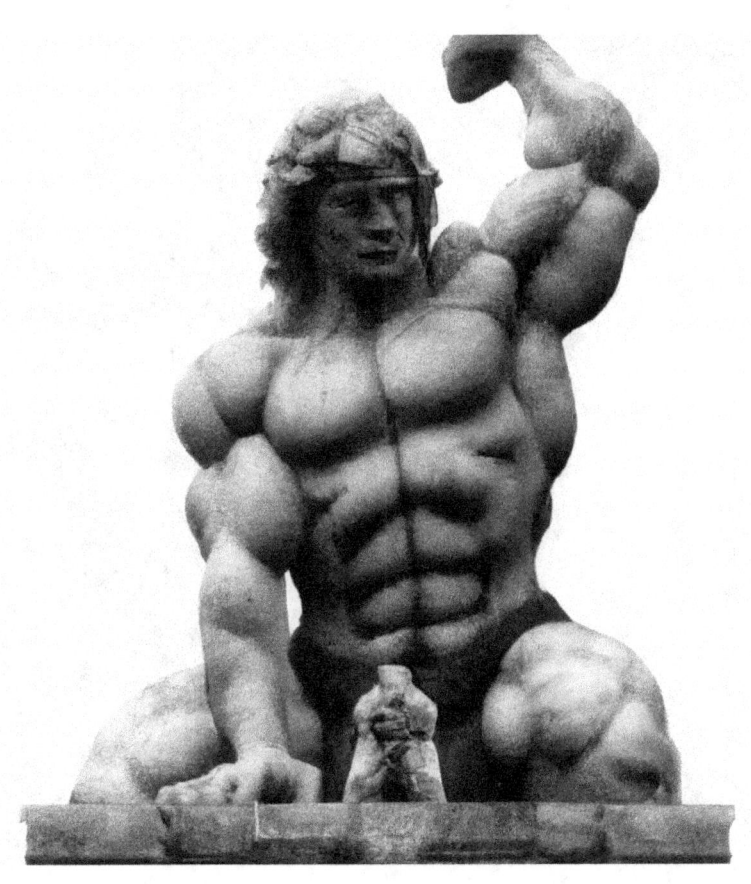

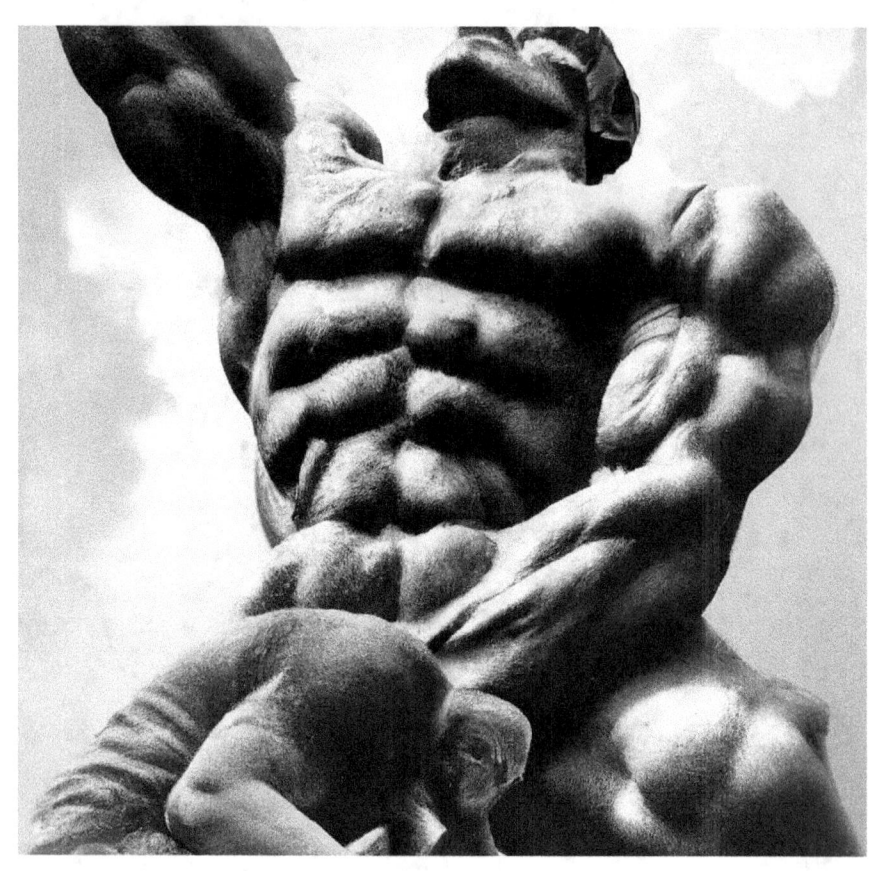

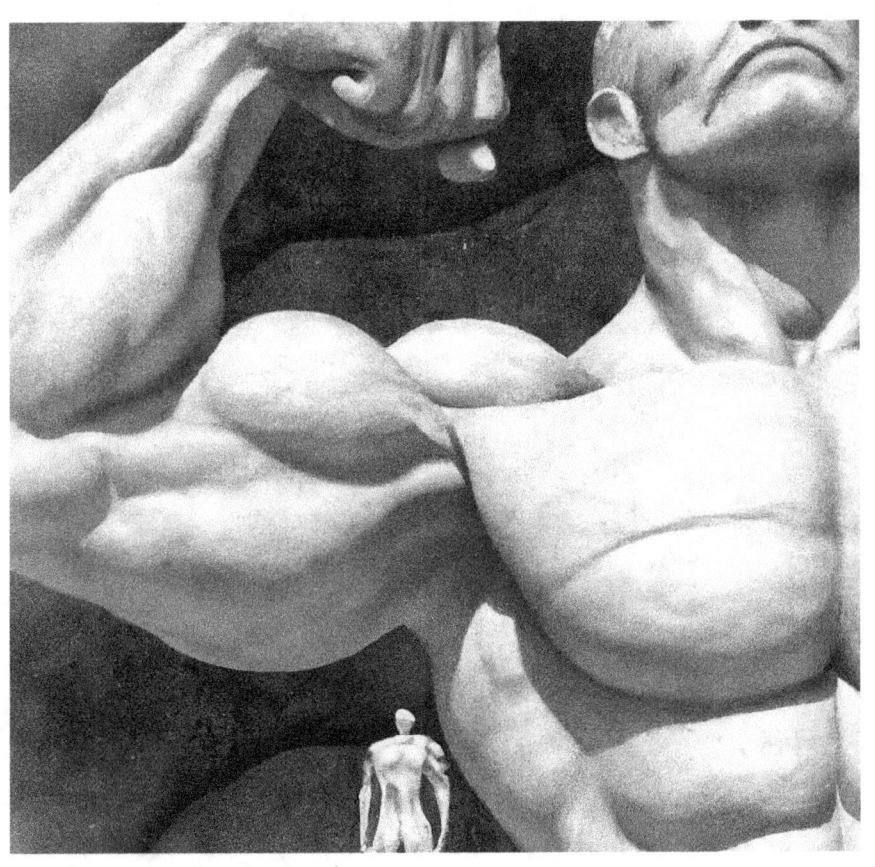

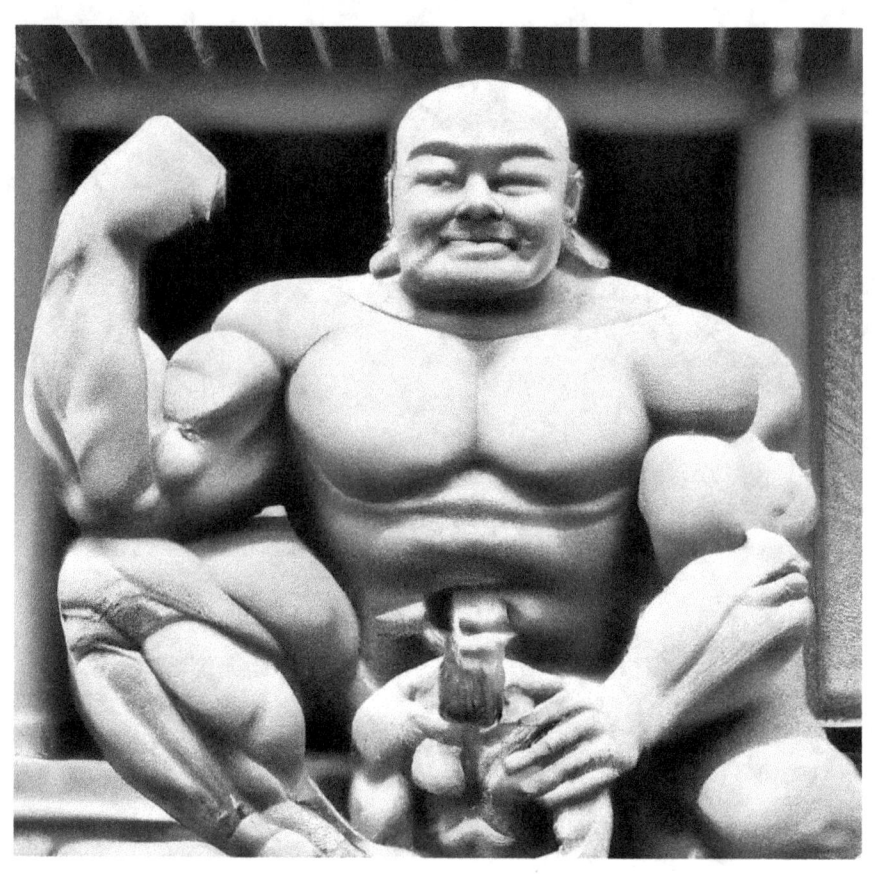

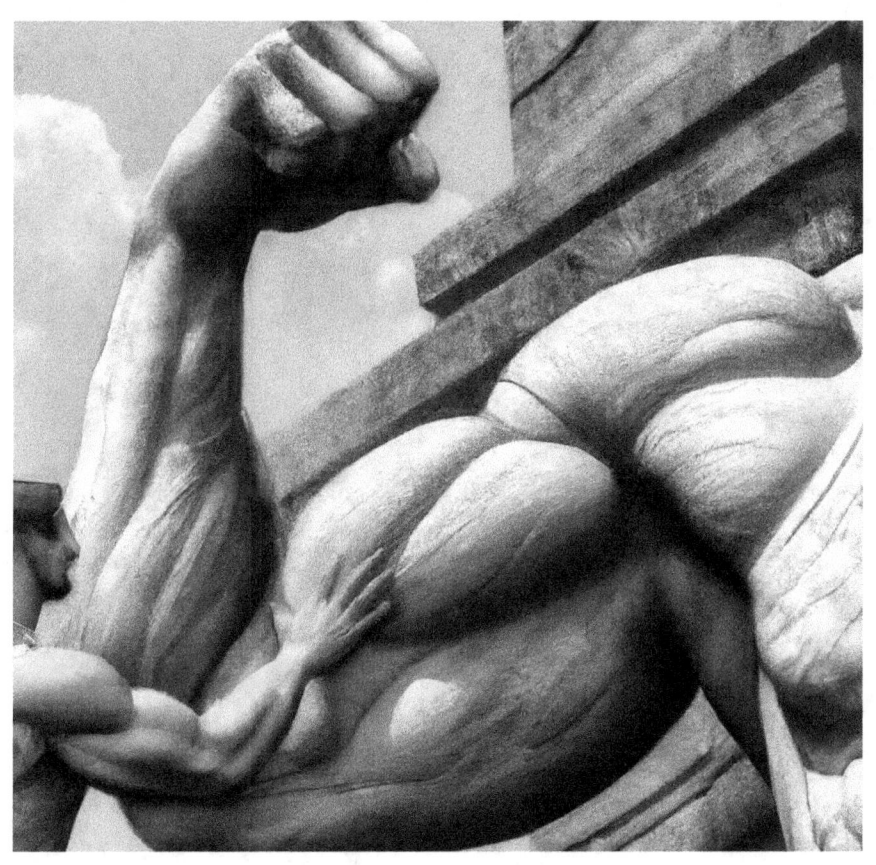

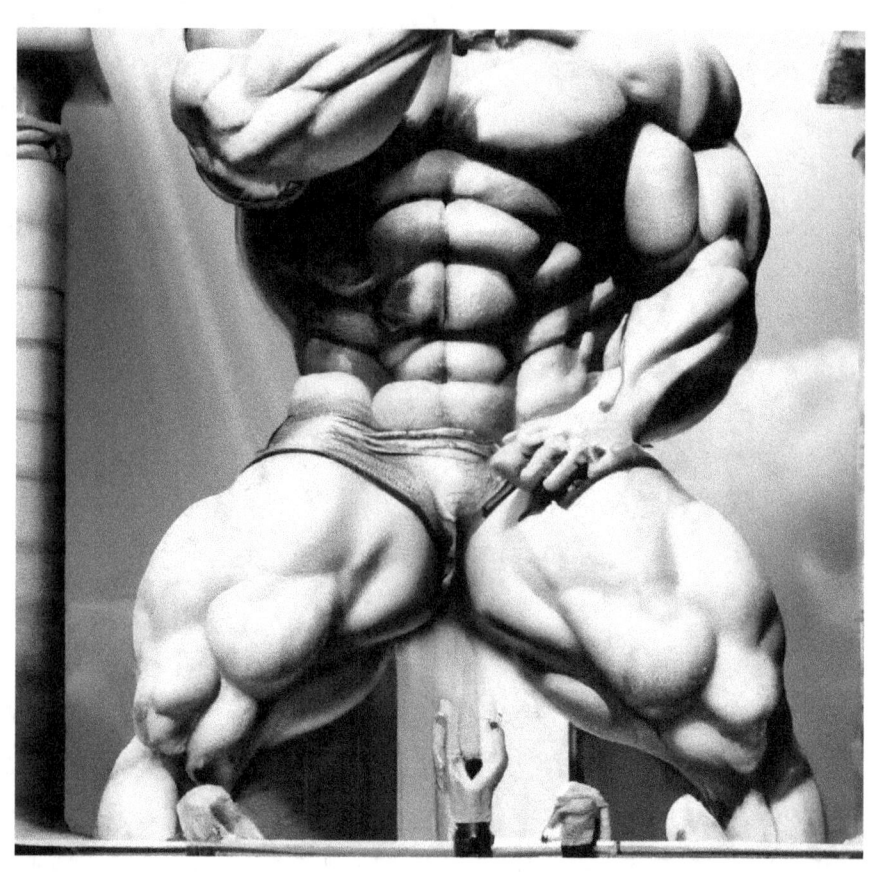

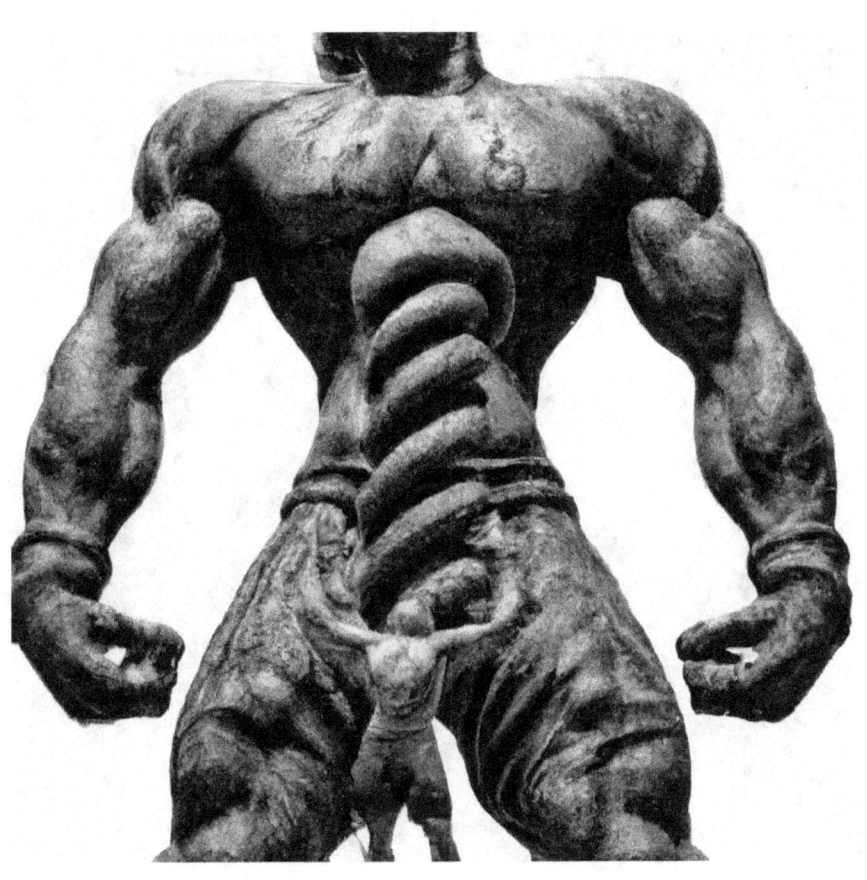

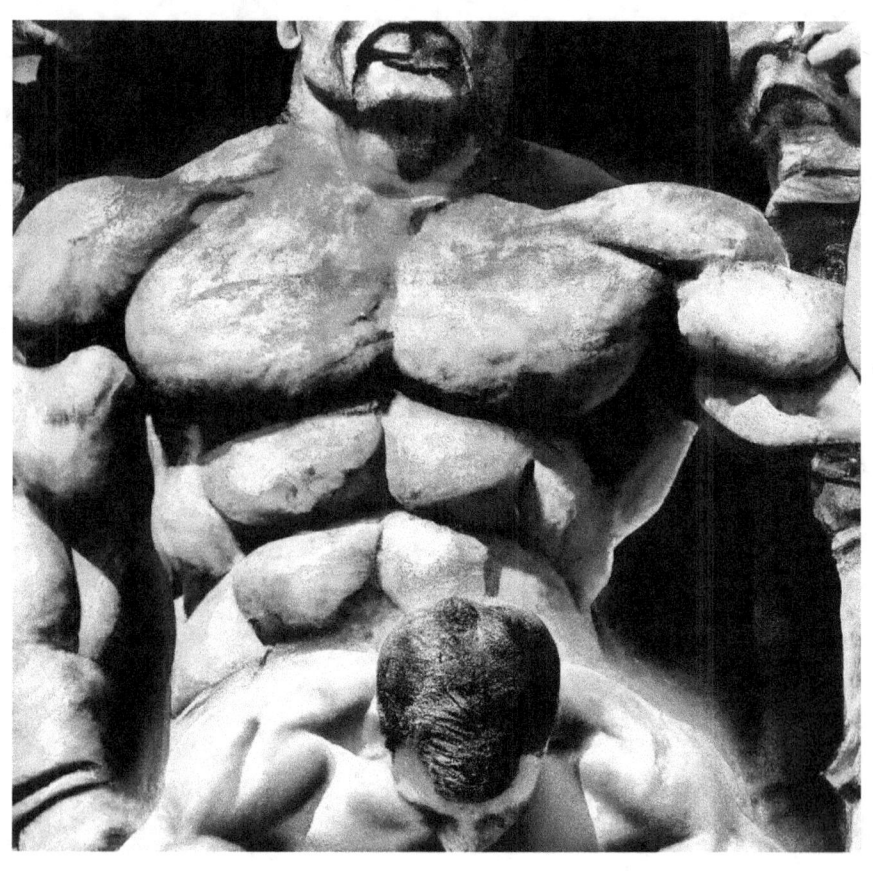

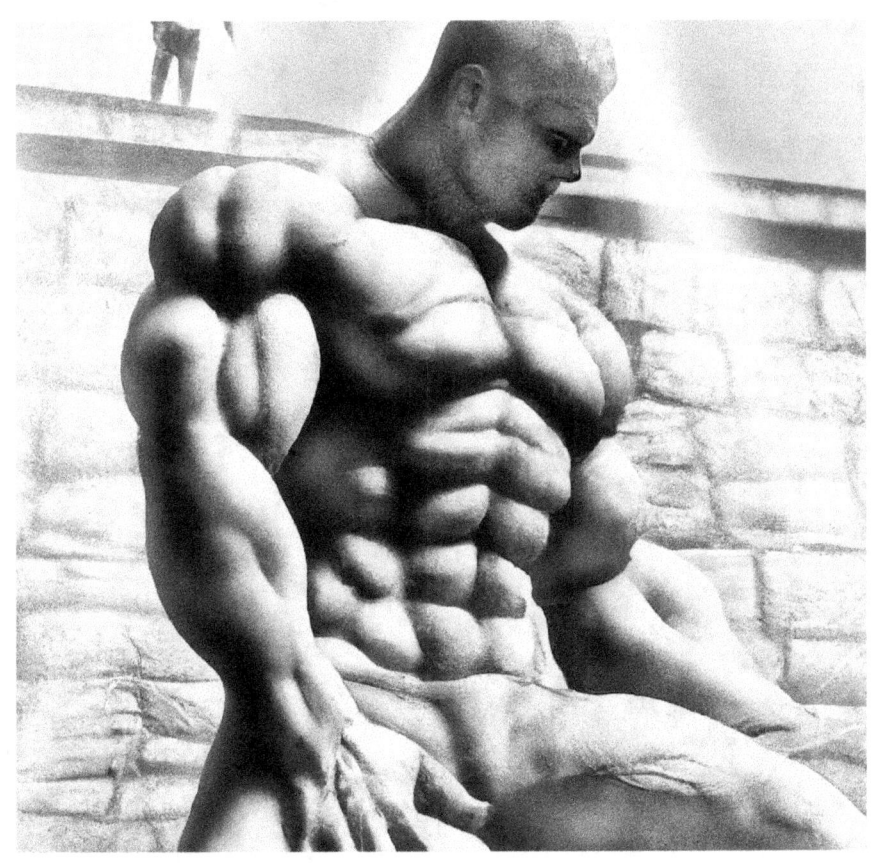

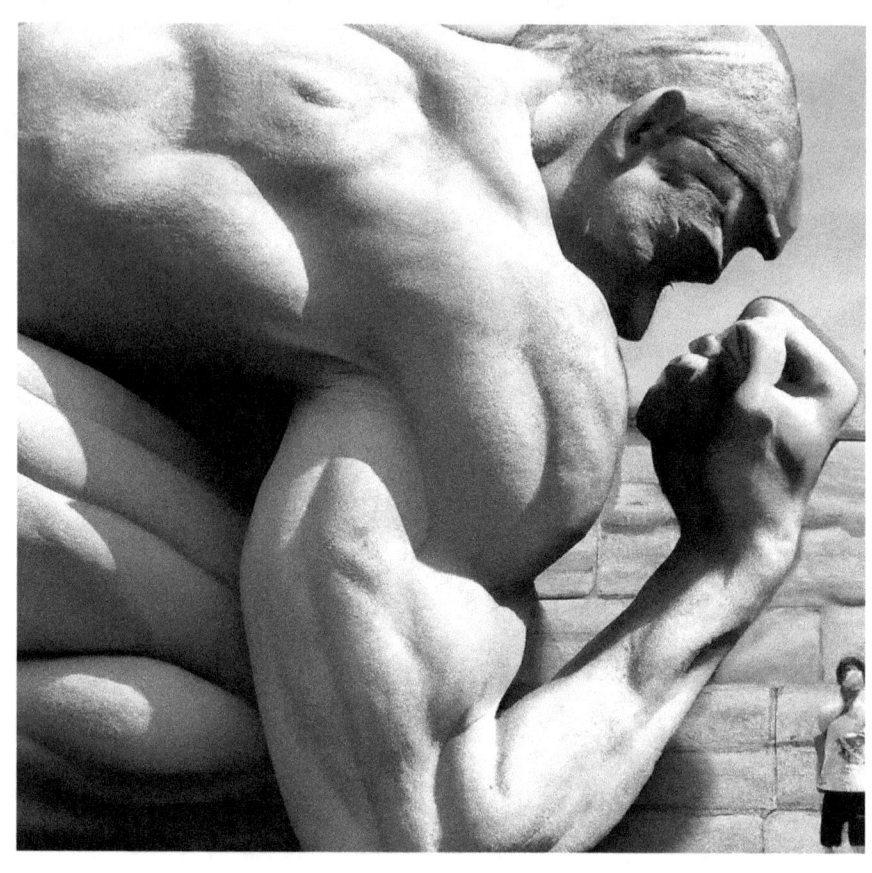

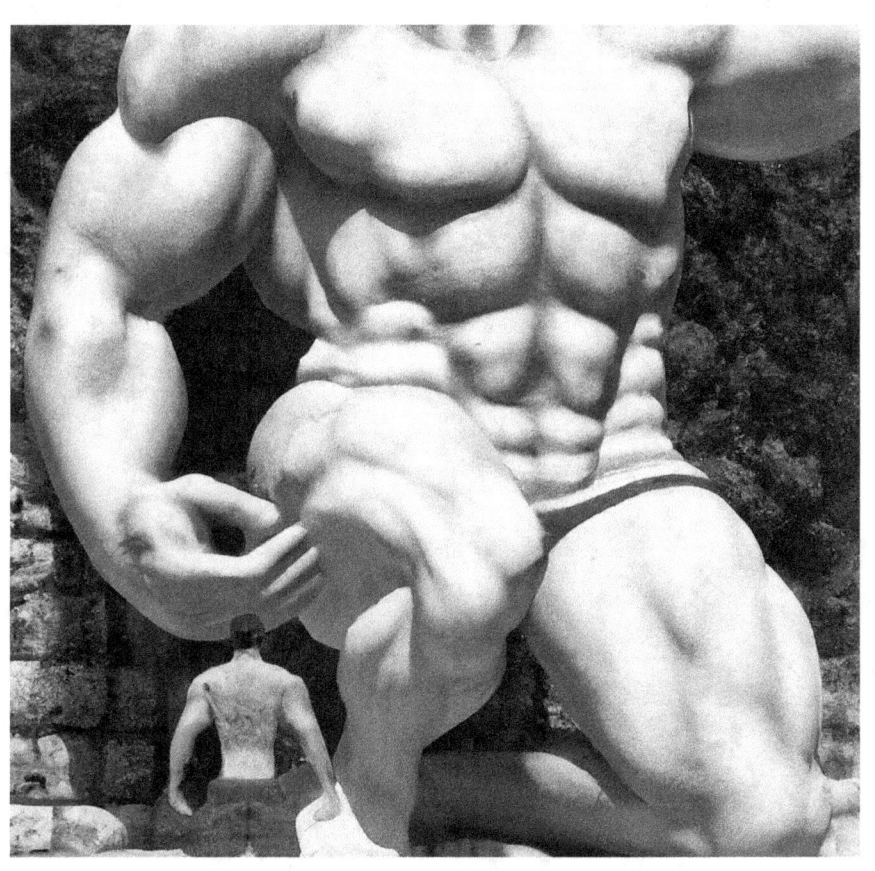

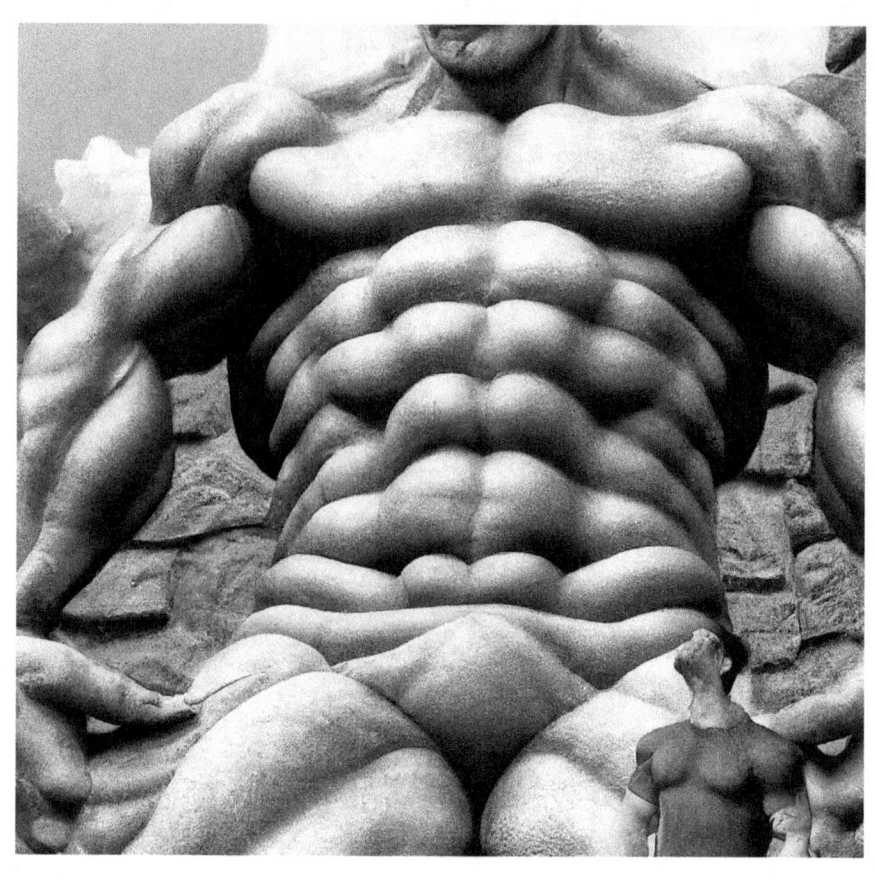

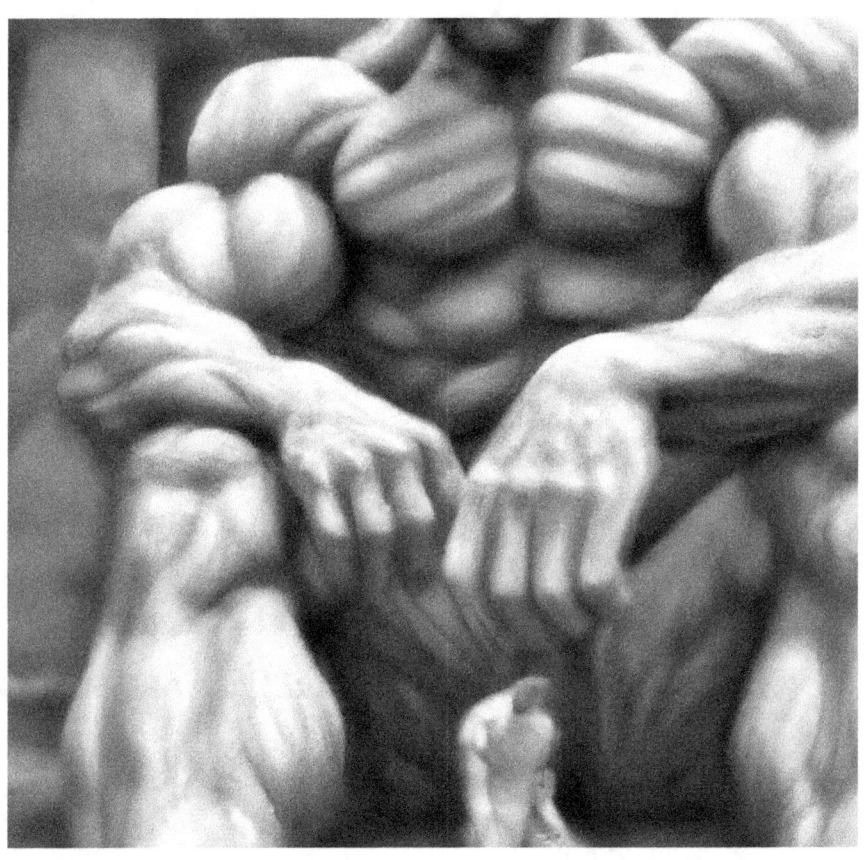

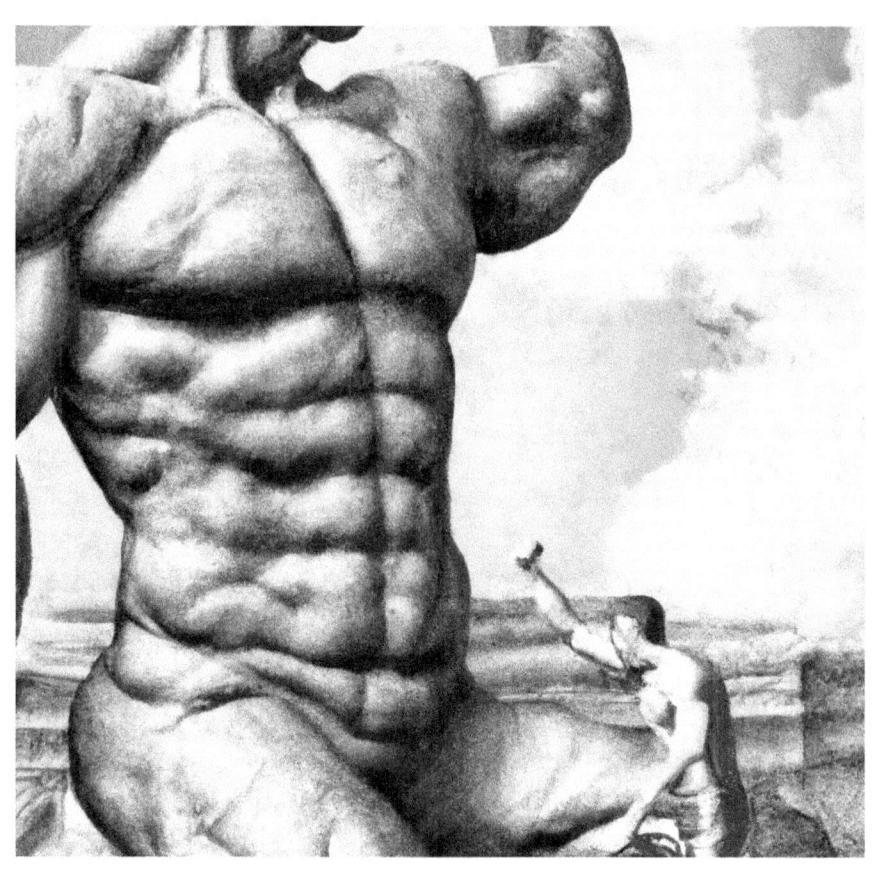

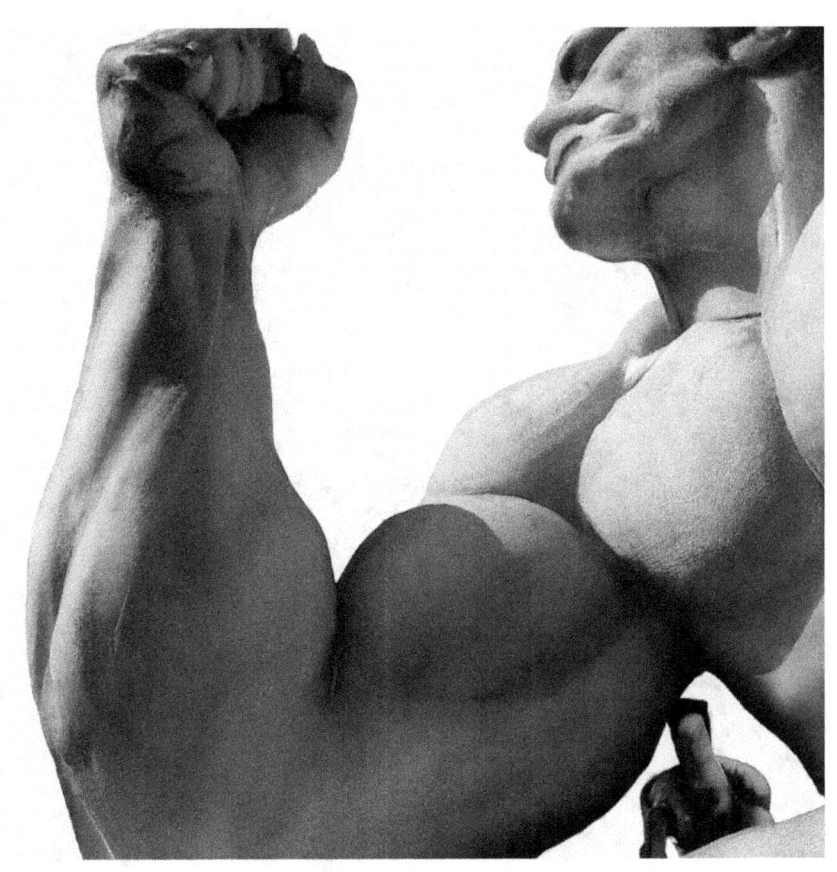

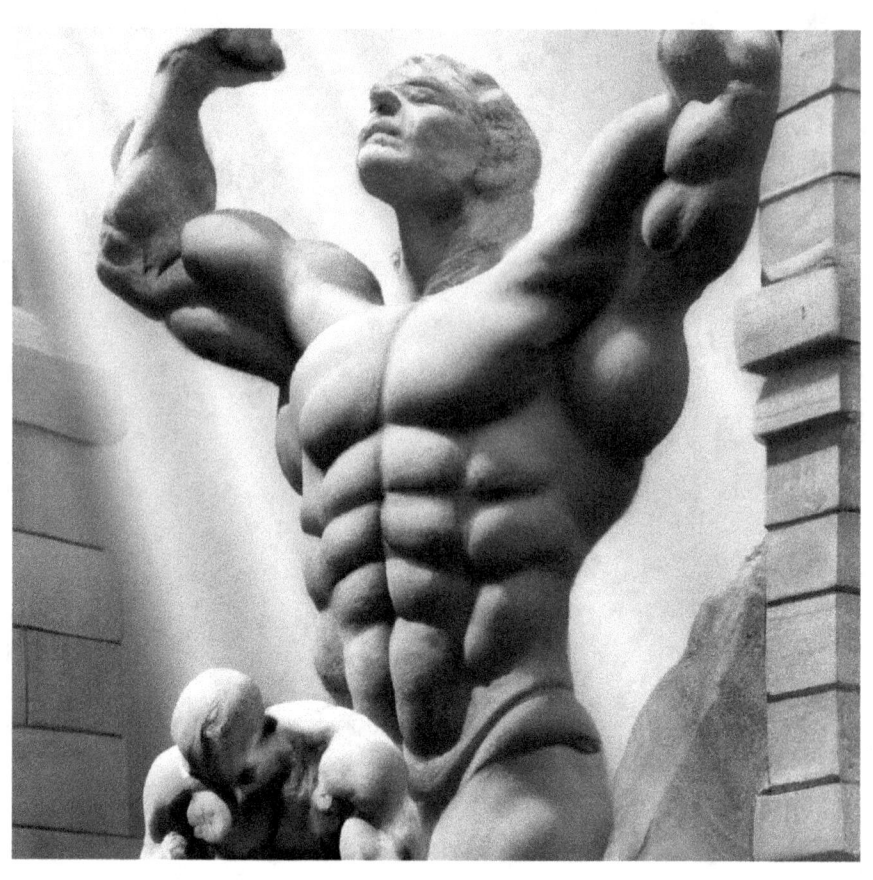

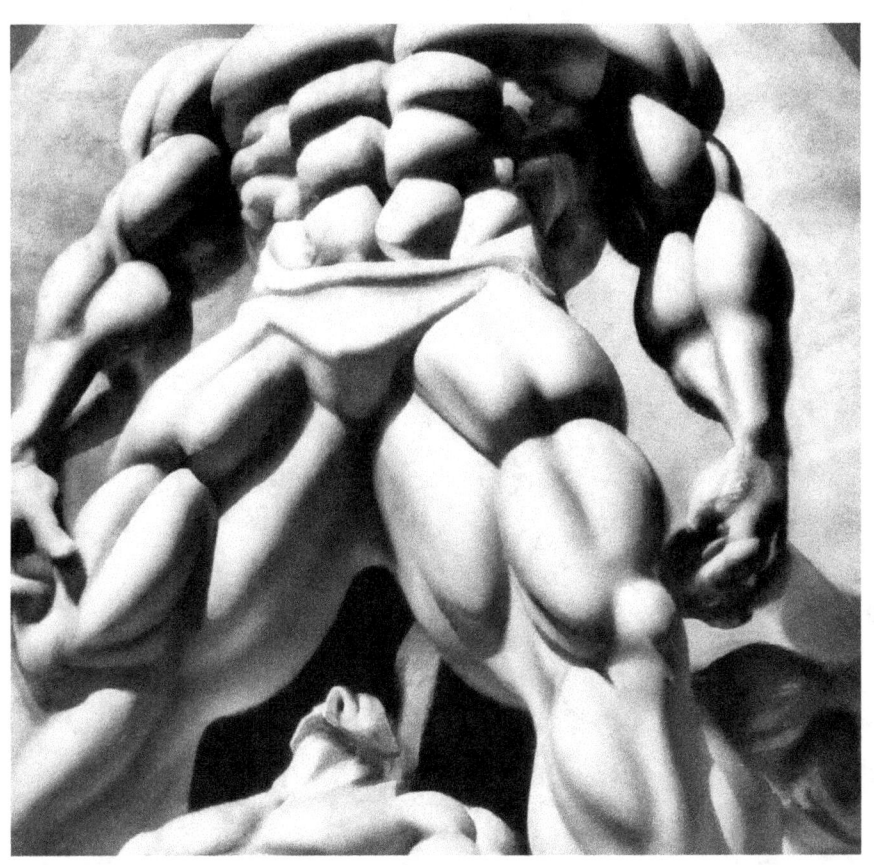

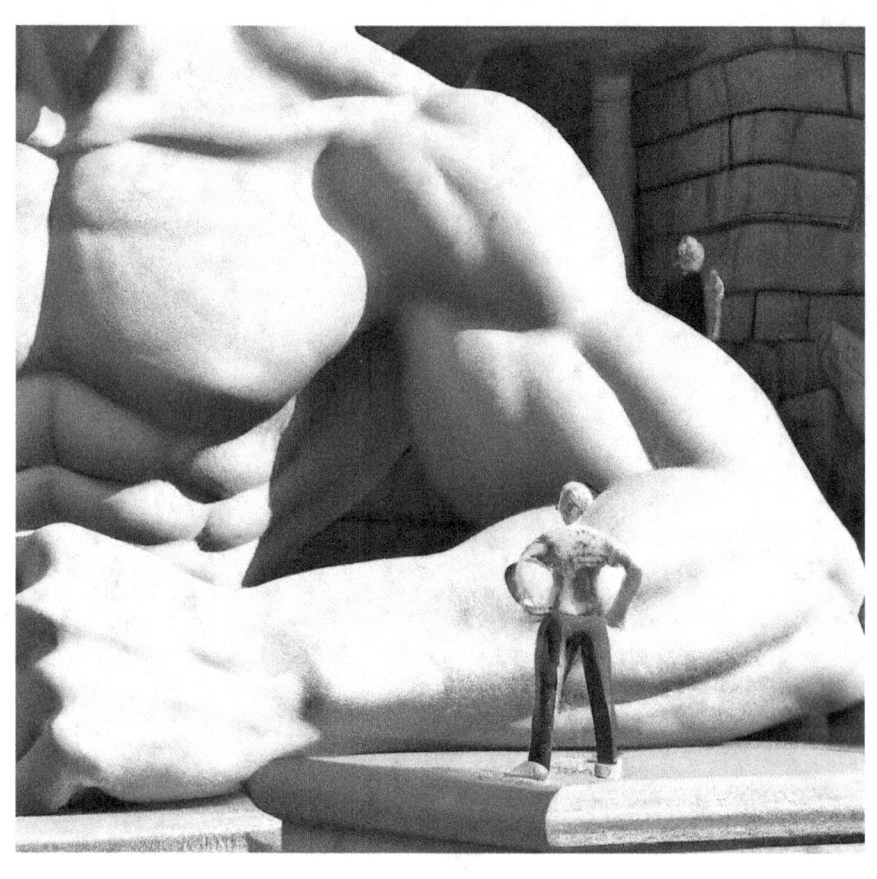

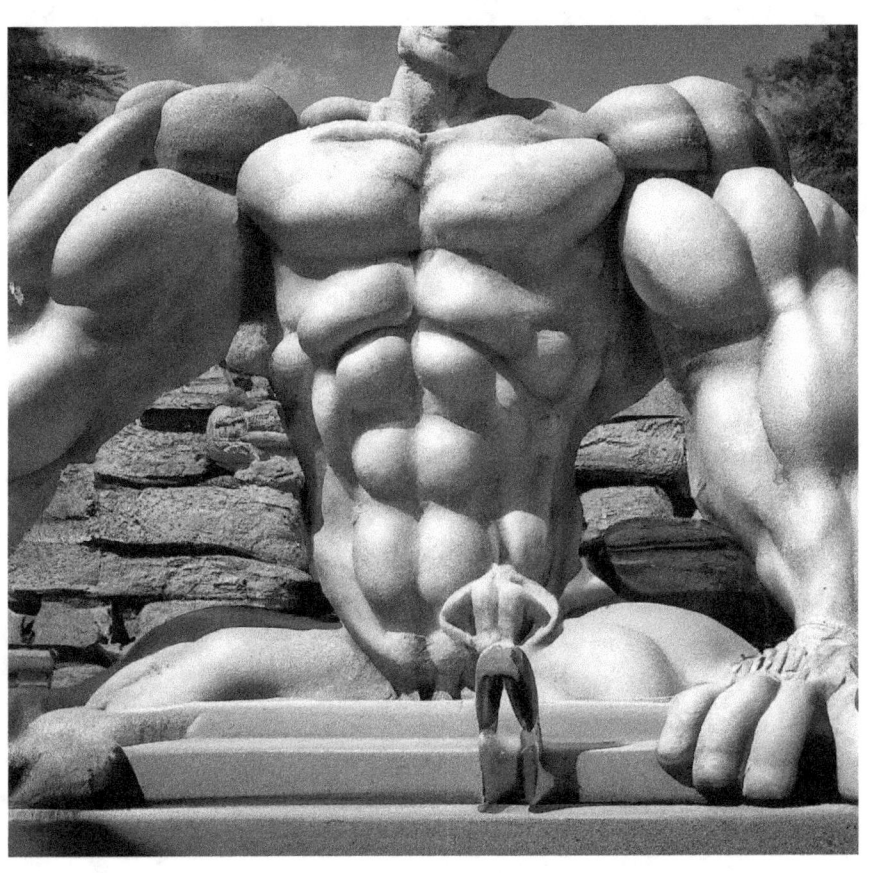

www.ingramcontent.com/pod-product-compliance
Lightning Source LLC
Chambersburg PA
CBHW071413210526
45465CB00001B/375